MEDIEVAL THEATRE COSTUME

Medieval Costumes

Medieval Theatre Costume

A PRACTICAL GUIDE TO THE CONSTRUCTION OF GARMENTS

IRIS BROOKE A.R.C.A.

THEATRE ARTS BOOKS · NEW YORK

FIRST PUBLISHED 1967

THEATRE ARTS BOOKS

333 SIXTH AVENUE, NEW YORK 10014

© 1967 IRIS BROOKE

SECOND IMPRESSION 1969

Certain of the drawings in this book first appeared in the Second Edition of *Western European Costume, Volume I, 13th to 17th Centuries,* by Iris Brooke, published by Theatre Arts Books. Copyright © 1963 by Iris Brooke.

Library of Congress Catalog Card No. 67-25699

Printed in Great Britain

Contents

Illustrations

Illustrations PAGE

CHAPTER I

Introduction

There has long been a very real need for practical constructional help in the Theatre Wardrobe. Dressmakers trained in a modern school of dress design, where innumerable devices exist to help their speedy churning out of modern clothes with a minimum of material, have undertaken the almost impossible task of trying to make clothes for the stage in the same manner. The theatre is not in any way similar to reality or fashion, and the very nature of theatrical performance cries out for special attention to costume. Actors wearing their own everyday clothes are to all intents and purposes themselves, and are therefore hampered and not helped in their act of being another person. This is a problem which has to be faced for any modern play and one which unfortunately has rarely been properly overcome, but for a play taken from the past it should be a great deal easier because there is a certain pattern in history which sets a standard of design.

The wealthy, the gods, ecclesiastics and foreigners, to take but a few at random, have each an accepted code of dress which should make them immediately recognisable, thus helping the audience in their involvement in the play, as well as helping the actor in his gestures and characterisation.

There has been no period in history when contemporary clothes were quite so difficult to wear for dramatic purposes as they are today. They may be the perfect reflection of our present needs, but they do not help to create any sort of atmosphere, they give no sense either of dignity or of squalor, either of grace or disgrace. The theatre demands all these qualities and theatre costume should be designed to clarify the position of the actor.

With this in mind it should be an easier proposition to produce costumes that will adequately clothe and assist the actor who is attempting to play the part of an historical figure. It is not in the least necessary to copy from historical portraits the exaggerated detail which formed part of the personal exhibitionism of past patrons of the arts. Their portraits were painted for the admiring homage of a generation to come—a real show-off—rather than a costume worn for an everyday affair. This unfortunate inclination to consult portraits for designs for theatre costume is still indulged, due partly to the prevailing tendency to hire stock costume, but also to a complete misunderstanding of what a costume is supposed to do for an actor.

Perhaps we are still struggling against the so-called historical accuracy and archaeological exactitude preached by Charles Kean in the middle of the last century when he expected his designer, Shaw, to create designs taken entirely from portraits of the past. A glimpse at the publications of Shaw's drawings will show that there was much hard work involved but that there was a lamentably limited scope, and we can see his exact copies of certain 15th-century costumes depicted in the completed drawings of Kean's productions (Enthoven Collection at the Victoria and Albert Museum) standing side by side with the fairies in ballet costume, who were introduced into the production of *Henry V*.

Such an attitude towards the theatre should be dismissed as outmoded, just as other mannerisms of the 19th century have been discarded. We no longer have dozens of underpaid hands to create the fanciful costumes that Henry Irving wore (which are now to be seen in the London Museum, Kensington Palace); nor those of H. B. Irving. Hamlet dripping with black jet beads, for instance (see the Russell Cotes Museum, Bournemouth), but it is more than ever possible to create brilliant effects and sweeping lines if such trivial details can be overcome.

For any theatrical production—both professional and amateur—the three most important factors in the making of costumes are time, finance and fabric.

We are assuming that decent designs are already available, and that the designer who made them has some specialist knowledge of what can and what cannot be used with a limited budget. There are, of course, plenty of designers willing and eager to concoct lovely colour schemes and elegant drawings which require a very large budget indeed, coupled with the skilled work of dozens of people with unlimited time at their disposal. Unfortunately this happy state of affairs rarely exists, and it is as well from the onset to realise the practical limitations which must normally govern such undertakings.

Time is usually of primary importance; the time between the original casting and the appearance of a fitted and finished dress which will not only give the actor a sense of character, but will also make him feel that it is his costume for that particular part. This consideration is not fully appreciated because it happens frequently that a certain costume is still unfinished—for a dozen different reasons—at the first dress rehearsal, so that the actor never has a chance to identify his part with his costume. This problem will in all prob-ability create a sense of discomfort, quite apart from the normal physical

adjustments which are so very necessary to practise before anything approaching a decent performance can be expected. Another aspect of time is the actual
man-power working hours available for the making of the costumes—how
many willing hands with how many hours at their disposal? Particularly does
this apply to student groups and amateur companies, but it is also a problem
in the profession because of the thousand and one emergencies that may arise.
It is not enough for half a dozen willing but unskilled helpers to find the odd
hour between cooking the dinner and bathing the baby. Enthusiasm is a
useful quality, but concentration is a much better one.

Ideally, certain organised groups should be supervised by someone who
sees that not too much time is wasted; that the right people are doing those
things for which they are best suited; that the odd word here and there may
save hours of unnecessary unpicking; that the one person who is familiar with
the vagaries of a certain sewing-machine is not compelled to use one that
almost anyone can understand, leaving the peculiar one to become the
experimental plaything of various uninitiated helpers; to see that those people
with a gift for handling delicate things are in charge of the finer decorations,
jewel-setting, crowns and perhaps masks, but do not waste their precious time
in sewing on buttons or hooks and eyes.

Time again for considered shopping, not just a mad rush to the nearest and
probably most expensive store, but time to set down what exactly will be
needed, where such things can be easily accessible, some knowledge of the
difficulties to be met in wholesale establishments—the stores who will give
the best possible assistance and perhaps a few shillings off the normal price if
a considerable number of purchases are made; time to visit the second-hand
shops, markets and junk stores where suitable and often enchanting bits and
pieces can be found. All these excursions take a great deal of time, but the
reward is great and often out of proportion to the trouble taken, for usually
an inexpensive alternative is found to something that could cost a deal more
and be far less effective.

Finance is a restricting element, however much money there seems to be
before the production is started. It is possible to spend the lot all too easily,
and if the budget is a small one every possible contingency should be worked
out before a penny is spent. Given a certain sum of money, it is always necessary
to have some idea as to how this should be divided amongst the characters.
There is no need to lay out the greatest sums on the main characters, for it is
not always the most expensive costume that is the most dramatic. There are
several famous designers who specialise in searching far and wide in markets,
junk shops and auction sales for old materials such as curtains, bedspreads and
old crinoline skirts, not to mention actual ecclesiastical robes. The stage and

dramatic value of such trophies is far higher than that of any brand new man-made fabric, their colour often richer and more subtle. Even the faded marks give light and texture to the newly-fitted garment that no amount of spraying could achieve. It is the smaller, often unconsidered items such as linings and interlinings, stiffening, buckram, jewels and sequins, Copydex and Bostik and —most important of all—footwear and wigs that really makes holes in the budget.

Given the right hairstyle and the right sort of footwear, the battle is half won. Oxford shoes in a Greek chorus can wreck any show, however well it is produced, as can a crew-cut in a 'Restoration' comedy.

Such examples may appear fanciful to the reader, but I have seen both in productions which were put on for discriminating audiences, possibly from sheer carelessness but perhaps from complete blindness to the general visual effect. In both cases there were members of the audience who took exception to the production on these grounds. One cannot blame them.

Fabric, which must be chosen for its texture and suitability for the task it has to play, can do a very great deal to help the actor and the significance of the scene. Most modern fabrics have been introduced to fill the needs of a modern society which is continually on the move and has little or no time at its disposal to care for clothes that are worn for convenience's sake, rather than for decorative purposes. Drip-dry, non-crush, non-iron, light-weight, and easy to pack or throw into the washing-machine, colours such as will withstand the persecution of almost boiling water and the juxtaposition of other colours without fear of running or fading. Such fabrics are stocked normally today in pastel shades, or dyed with some brilliant aniline that might be vastly effective on its own, perhaps lying on a beach, but was not designed to fit into a colour scheme that would be most effective in a theatre.

The fabrics with both texture and colour significance are not easy to find, and unless such materials as furnishing fabrics, hessian, crash and perhaps old blankets are looked upon as having the right sort of weight and the right draping effects, the performance will become hampered by the age in which we live.

One fascinating experience in New York showed me that the problem was no always being reasonably handled there. A designer, who was putting on a show in Central Park, in a hot and unbelievably suffocating summer, stated that his costumes were designed 'in the English manner', and proceeded to inform his audience that the tradition in England was to make all the Shake-spearean clothes with a felt lining 'thus giving them body and strength'. Perhaps some of the Stratford costumes are treated in this way, but it is cold in this country and the actors would not be unduly taxed by a felt lining.

Central Park in the heat of the summer has a temperature often up in the nineties, and it gets no cooler in the evening. It is not necessary to burden any actor with the weight of his clothes as long as the right line can be achieved. A chain in the hem of a train can give as much dignity to that train as if it were made from ermine and velvet.

With these three major problems under control, there is one outstanding snag to overcome. How do we start to make clothes without patterns? The answer must come from the past itself, before there were such things as sewing-machines and paper-patterns, even before there were professional tailors: beautiful clothes were designed and carried out with a maximum of simplicity and a minimum of waste. This was an art just as much as any other art, and those who were so talented enjoyed the achievement of something very near perfection.

The scale drawings and diagrams in this book should give a clue, not too hard to follow, to the elements of such construction.

A 13th-century Squire.

The rest of the book deals entirely with such necessary subjects as colour significance, emblems and insignia, properties, simple head-dress, the hood and cloak, long hose, shoes, crowns and coronets, wings and swords; simple rules for measuring, cutting, lining, printing, and an easy effect for embroideries. In fact all those endless little things that can help to make or mar a production from the visual point of view.

Such things as masks (for devils), armour and helmets are not simple either to make or to explain, and unless the company concerned has some artist with time and patience at his disposal, they can be a lot more trouble than the finished effect justifies. It is always possible to hire a good suit of armour at a price which compares favourably with the time and materials required to make one. Masks are fairly easy if you have the gift, and a few hints and suggestions for materials are given in the section dealing with properties.

DIAGRAMS OF MEASUREMENT

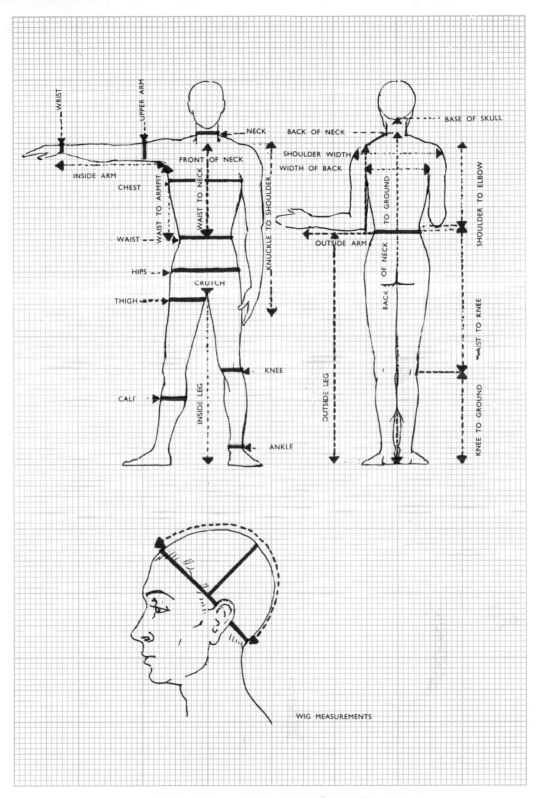

1. Essential measurements and where to take them.

SCALE: ONE INCH TO A SQUARE

HEAD—ONE INCH TO THREE SQUARES

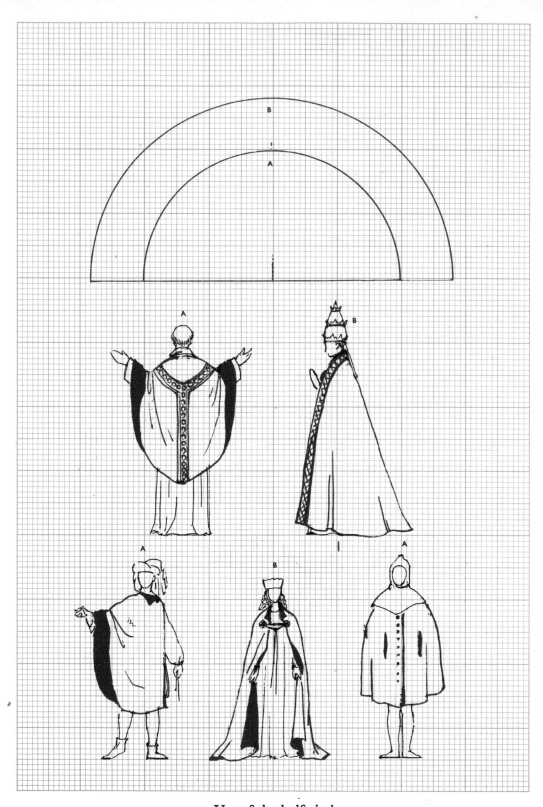

2. Use of the half circle.

SCALE: TWO INCHES TO A SQUARE

3. Use of the half circle. (Dotted line indicates cutting for A and C).

SCALE: TWO INCHES TO A SQUARE

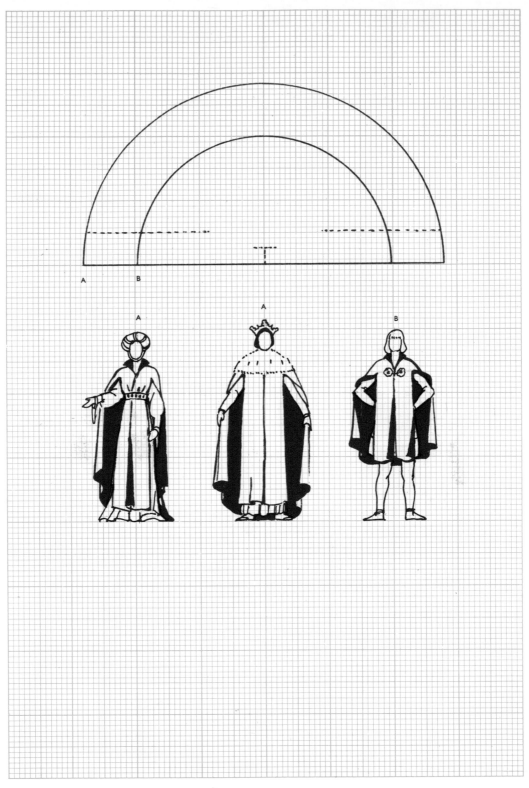

4. Use of the half circle cut with front panels.

SCALE: TWO INCHES TO A SQUARE

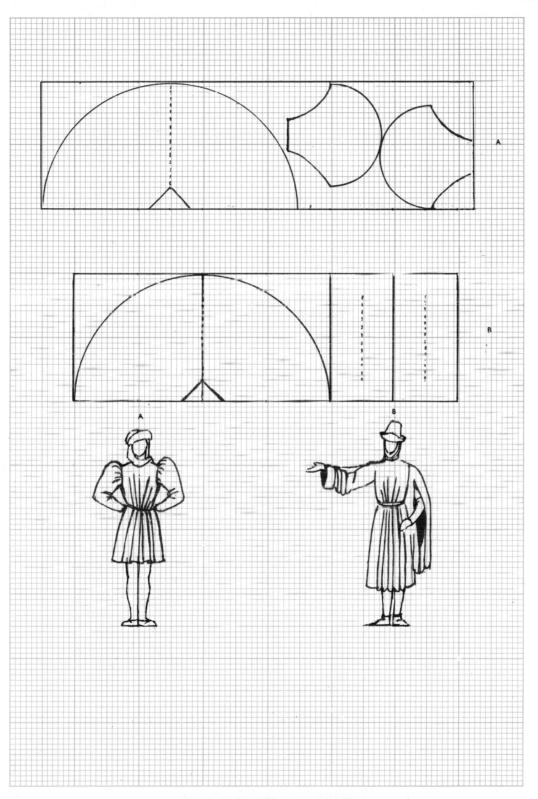

5. Half circle with sleeves added.

SCALE: TWO INCHES TO A SQUARE

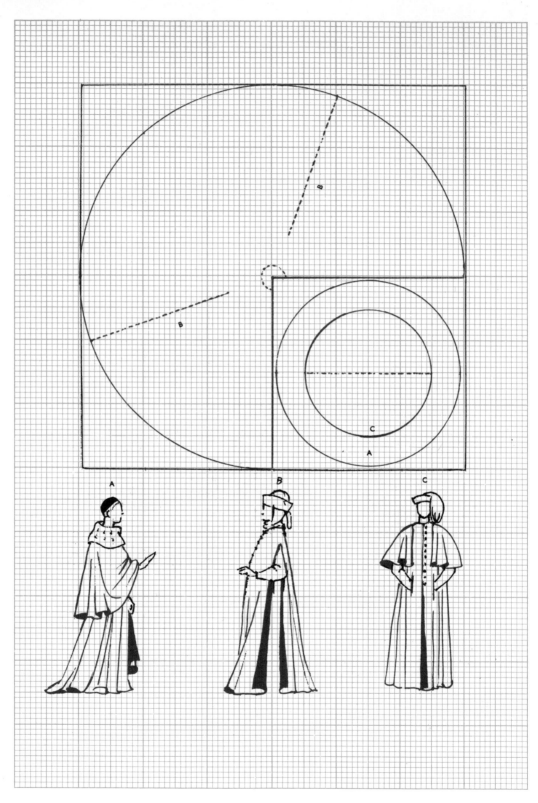

6. Three-quarter circle and circular cape or cap sleeve.

SCALE: TWO INCHES TO A SQUARE

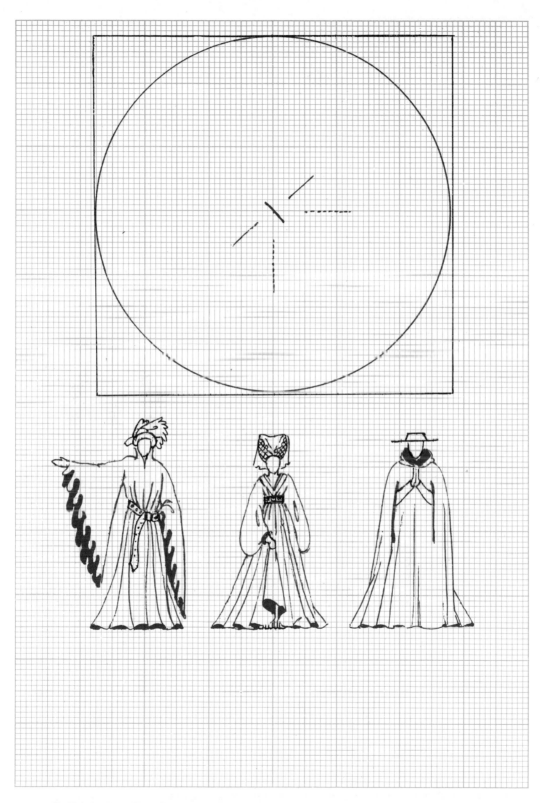

7. Full circle. (Sections outside circle can be used as sleeves. Dotted lines indicate Cardinal's arm openings).

SCALE: TWO INCHES TO A SQUARE

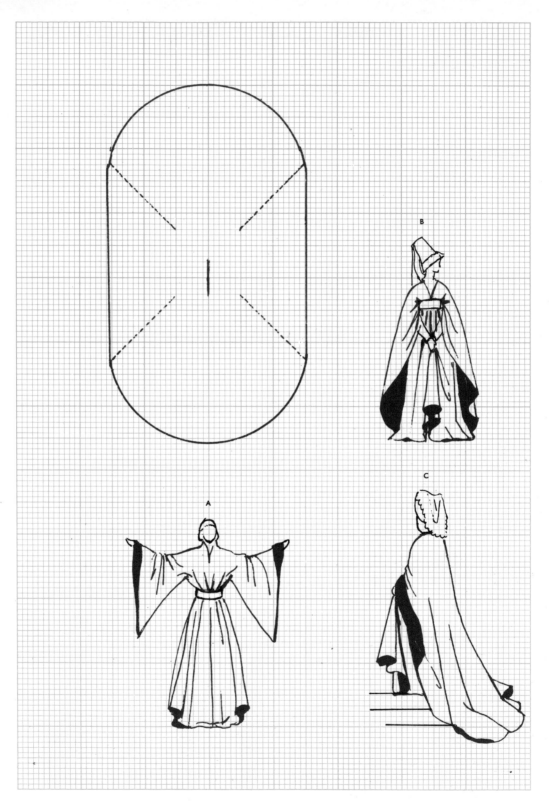

8. Oval with straight sides. (Dotted line for man's sleeve only).

SCALE: TWO INCHES TO A SQUARE

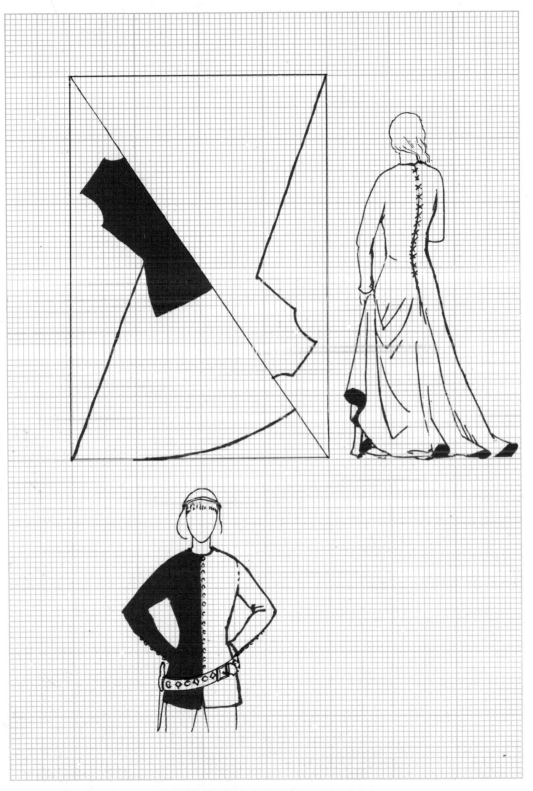

9. Diagram for cutting fitted garments.

SCALE: ONE INCH TO A SQUARE

10. Diagram for sleeveless gown.

SCALE: ONE INCH TO A SQUARE

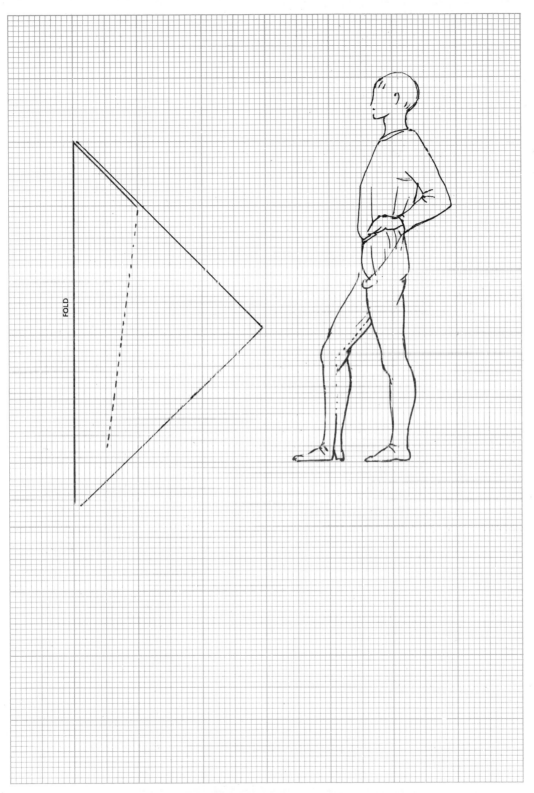

FOLD

11. Simplified hose. (Lower leg and foot to be fitted).

SCALE: ONE INCH TO A SQUARE

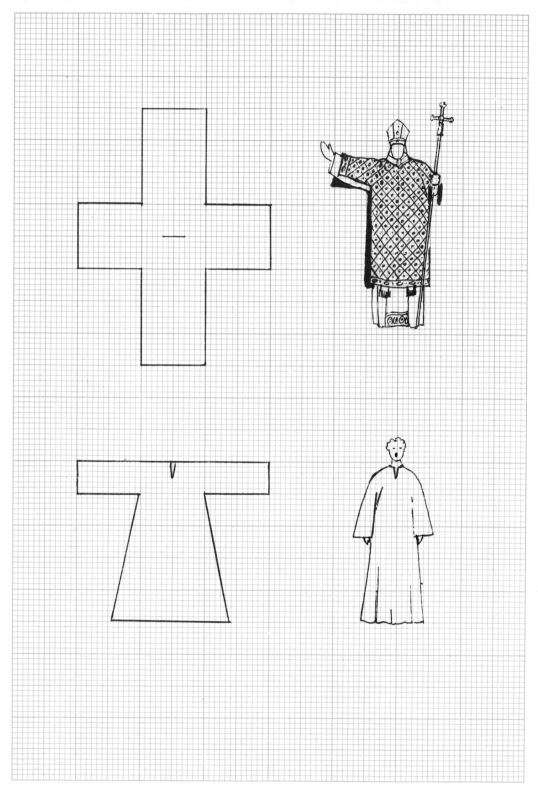

12. Dalmatic and alb.

SCALE: TWO INCHES TO A SQUARE

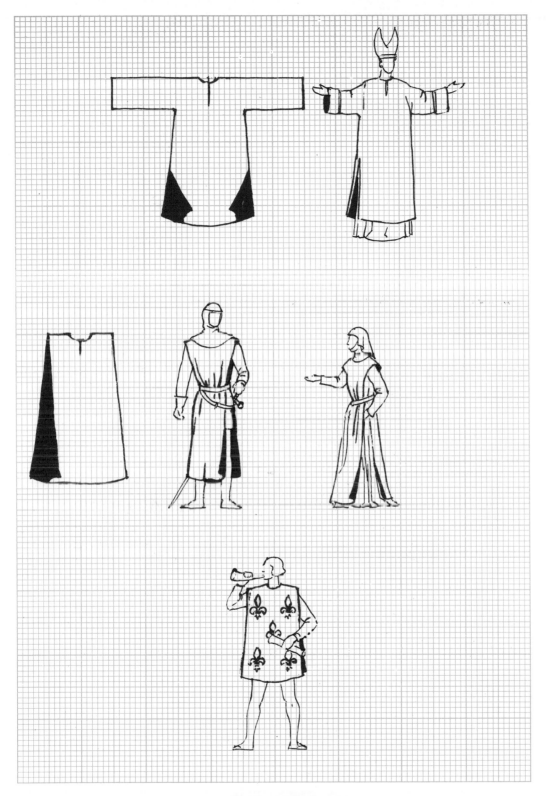

13. Tunic and tabard.

SCALE: TWO INCHES TO A SQUARE

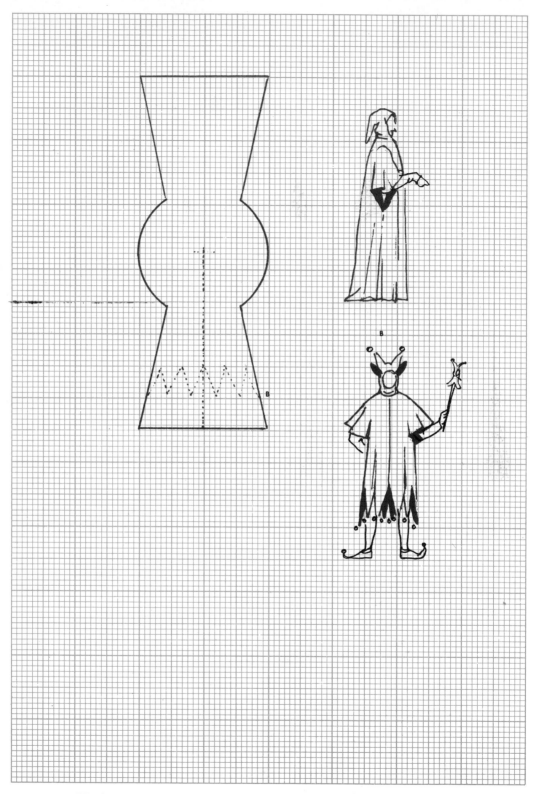

14. Variations on caped gowns. (Hoods can be made from segments).

SCALE: TWO INCHES TO A SQUARE

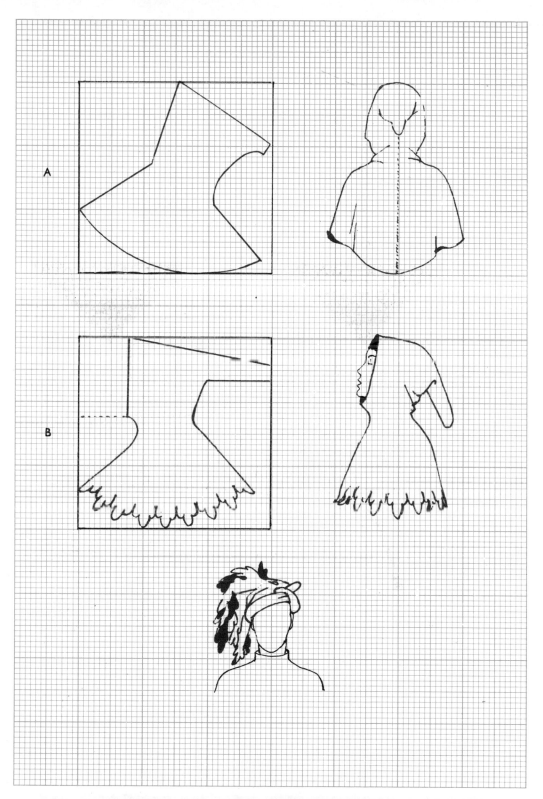

15. Hoods and final use as hat. (Dotted line on B indicates possible turn-back or cuff).

SCALE: ONE INCH TO A SQUARE

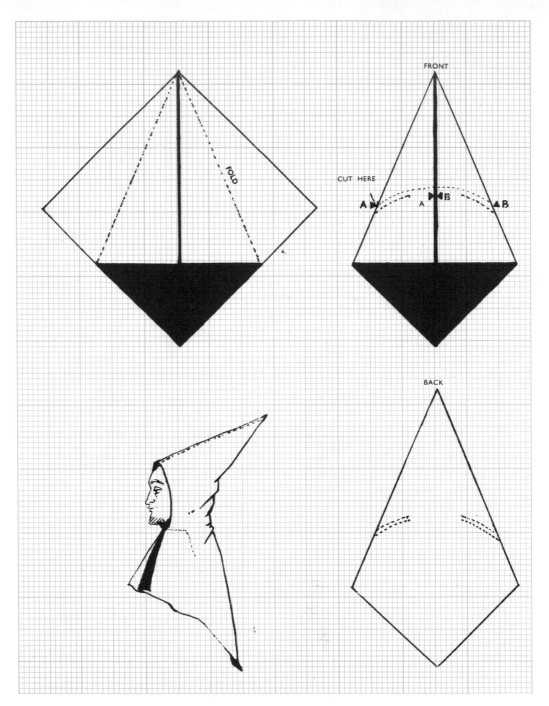

16. Hood made from diagonal square.

SCALE: ONE INCH TO A SQUARE

This particular drawing needs some explanation. The first diagram indicates where the fold·must be turned onto a centre line, leaving a point at the back (shown as solid red). The second shows the front of the hood and the black dotted line where the front *only* is to be cut. Red dots are at the *back*. Points marked A and B in the front must be turned back to join A and B at the sides. Black dots on the third drawing show how this should appear when it is sewn together. It is advisable to experiment with a small square of paper to familiarise oneself with its simplicity and effectiveness.

CHAPTER 2

Wardrobe

Experience over the last dozen years or more, working on productions for which students and theatre wardrobes were expected to attack all problems of design and costume on a shoe-string budget (making use of a great deal of practically useless materials), has made it increasingly clear to me that a stock wardrobe can be a very real nuisance and a dreadful waste of time and patience: one year you may be coping with a race of young giants and the next with not a soul over 5 ft. 10 in.! To a certain extent this applies to almost any company because it is impossible to select actors and actresses of an even reasonably good quality if their size has to be taken into consideration. A young man of 6 ft. 4 in. (and there seem to be a great many of these today) cannot be expected to look dignified and imposing if he is wearing a cope, however beautiful, that has been used by another of 5 ft. 10 in., nor is there any practical method of lengthening such a garment without utterly wrecking the grace of the original half-circle. Length of garments is of the very greatest importance, especially if such plays are to be performed in a church. Skimpy clothes look mean, and curiously enough both modern and wrong; the sweeping hems of circular and semi-circular garments do much to enhance the dramatic value of the production, making lovely pools of colour when the actor is still, and creating a sense of age and grace in movement.

Let us assume, then, that we are in the happy position of starting from scratch, and are not hampered at the commencement of a production by having to use old clothes made for other people for another production, but have a free hand to work from our own collection of designs and fabrics.

It is fortunate for our purpose that the basic garments of the Middle Ages, particularly the 14th and 15th centuries, were mostly planned so that there was a minimum of wasted fabric, a maximum of comfort and a rich variety of ideas in decoration that did not in any way interfere with the basic simplicity of cut. If we think of the clothes in the past as being the work of the housewife, rather than that of a professional tailor, it was clearly sensible and thrifty for her to make the very best use of the fabric available, which was either homespun with infinite labour, or else extremely costly. Such a simplicity and economy of cut will still give a beauty of line, a sweep and swing that is well-nigh impossible to imitate in a garment which has a complexity of seams, each and every one adding to the work of the wardrobe and often causing unnecessary stretching and clumsy easing which will ruin the hang, and which no amount of pressing will disguise.

The exceptions to this rule of simplicity were those clothes purposely made complicated by a tailor, and often such outlandish costumes have attracted the eye and been copied again and again, so that they have eventually become recognised as normal fashions rather than the unusual and extravagant habits that they were in their own time. Let us, therefore, assume that the ordinary people followed the economy of their parents and wore such robes as could be cut from handwoven fabrics with as little waste as possible.

This rule of simplicity, when put into practice, will make the whole problem of dressing cheaply a very much easier one for the modern production.

The richer clothes of the Middle Ages were often made from foreign material, for England at least could not manufacture silks and velvets; such luxuries came from the southern countries where it was possible to cultivate silk-worms. The riches of the northern countries came from wool and this was particularly English. Fine lawns and linens all had to be imported from the Continent, and it was not until the 17th century that we find records of the growing of flax for linen introduced into these islands. All through the 15th century rich garments were treated as very great treasures, handed down from father to son or bequeathed to friends and relations with as much care as the fine gold utensils and the beds and bedding. Such things were precious and not the necessary day-to-day requirements of the ordinary people. Therefore it would be only the wealthy and extravagant who appeared in the really new and fashionable garments; clothes here were 'dagged' and 'punched' and lined with fur, as Chaucer writes about them in *The Parson's Tale*.

It is not necessary to indulge in such fashions for the majority of miracles and mystery plays, but of course there are exceptions as well as the exotic characters in many of the moralities. Characters such as Worldly Riches, Covetousness, etc., would always require some outstanding dress to distinguish character and make them immediately recognisable to the audience. For this purpose the last chapter in this book has been added, giving simple instructions on the easiest way to achieve such an effect without investing too much time or money in the final costume.

A few words here may be of considerable help to the most comfortable method of working on any one production. It is as well for everyone to bear in mind that a wardrobe mistress's job is not to do the actual sewing. Her real chore is the complete organisation of the 'willing hands'. Perhaps she may be familiar with dressmaking, and let me say very emphatically that this particular ability is not what is really needed in theatre wardrobe. Tucks and darts, gores and gussets, odd cuffs and collars can be a dreadful waste of time, and to a great extent they are products of a more recent age and do little to enhance the costume of the Middle Ages.

The qualifications of a wardrobe mistress are ingenuity, imagination, an ability to make people co-operate, and a small working knowledge of how to interpret designs. Perhaps it is useful to have some sense of historical design, but this can be had from any little book dealing with the history of costume. Organisation is the real key-note of the exercise; but patience and a sense of humour must predominate.

The wardrobe itself must never be left in a state of chaos, whatever the urgency of other distractions. If it is, there are likely to be hours wasted looking for things, and the very fact of an urgent call means that many workers are quite likely to carry bits and pieces away with them that are essential to some particular costume. Someone must cope with this kind of emergency exit.

Don't crowd the wardrobe; leave space for cutting out however busy you may be. Every time you stop work for the day see that one person is always in charge of clearing up and seeing that everything used gets put back in its proper place. It is safer to have scissors on a loop of string and to hang them up whenever they are out of use; they tend to get lost or taken away quicker than anything else. Keep a magnet handy for sweeping the floor every now and then: the number of needles and pins you will find will be quite astounding. It is better to keep pins in a small tin than a cardboard box, as they don't get upset quite so easily, and if the tin is small enough it will not collect an assortment of minute junk such as beads, buttons, etc., which normally find their way into pin boxes, and are infuriating when you are groping for the next pin and cannot take your eyes off the garment you are trying to arrange.

Tack everything before machining, especially if cut on the cross or bias of the material. In cases where the fabric is stretchy, it is a very great help to sew over a sheet of newspaper so that the shuttle does not pull the fabric at all. The paper can be ripped off and used again at the end of each seam.

Just as soon as the cast list is made out measurements must be taken. Some means of contact with rehearsals and the wardrobe must be arranged, so that should a member of the cast fall out for any reason and be replaced by someone else the wardrobe is informed at once. All designs must be available for the producer to see before they are cut out, to give time to change such a design, should his idea be entirely different regarding some character. Some

producers see things in their mind's eye without being able to express themselves, and here it is very important that the designer does not interfere by
obstinately sticking to his original idea to the detriment of the production as a
whole. It is almost impossible to design for certain people without knowing
their limitations.

All the arts must be considered if we are to do justice to drama. Supreme
sensitivity to the actor's own problems will make for a better costume than
something straight from a design which has, perhaps, not been thought of at
all except as a little fragment of some scene. It is therefore the very essence of a
wardrobe mistress's job to see all the performers as often as possible. Sometimes
the actors are tiresome and insensitive, believing they can bully anyone into
thinking the way they do; an actor or actress who finds his or her costume
unmanageable and does not intend to make use of it, or a head-dress which
the intended wearer thinks unbecoming, though it may be perfect for the part
—these problems must be tactfully overcome.

There are a few practical instructions which at first sight appear so simple
and obvious that there might seem no necessity to explain them. But there are
a great many willing hands whose owners are not necessarily aware of some
simple facts that can be all too easily overlooked.

Measuring, lining and pressing are the most important tasks that should be
stressed, and if the costumes are to be of use in the future for other actors and other
productions it is impossible to over-emphasise the necessity for lining and pressing
throughout the process of making up. No seams should be left unpressed in
the hope that time can be saved by one lot of pressing instead of several;
each seam should be finished completely before the next one is undertaken.

Measuring carefully is, of course, the very first step in the procedure. On
page 17 minute instructions are given for carrying this out. It is not necessary
to take all the measurements suggested if the actor is not likely to play another
part within a comparatively short space of time. People's measurements do
change, and an actor whose chest is, say, 38 in. in the spring may quite easily
be 40 in. the autumn if he takes part in some strenuous exercise during the
summer. Common sense should govern the taking of such measurements so
that should he be wearing a long robe to the ground, time is not wasted in
taking calf measurements, thigh, or waist to knee, etc. These things are often
done in an excess of enthusiasm, but if time is precious a little thought beforehand will save a great deal of energy and patience.

The first essential in measuring is to establish the exact places on a given
person where the measuring points are. A string tied round the middle will
naturally slip to the normal waist, and this is the most important measuring
centre. Hips are normally placed some 7 in. below the waist, but this is not a

safe assumption: some women have their widest part much lower down, some only about 4 in. below the waist. Hip measurements should reveal the widest measurement, otherwise no end of trouble may arise from a tightly fitted garment. Chest measurements should be taken with the lungs filled, not deflated, and again at the widest place.

Always leave half an inch free on all measurements; it is easier to take in a seam than to let it out. Don't be persuaded that a girl's waist is 23 in. against a 25-in. measurement; it may easily be 2 in. different at some time or other, but the chances are that when the garment is made the 2 in. are needed. Never pull the tape-measure tight. Always double check in case you have the tape-measure twisted, inside-out or upside down. Should common sense make you hesitate over a certain measurement, just check again.

The point at the back of the neck is taken from the 5th vertebra, which is usually a trifle more prominent than those above. The front of the neck is the point between the collar bones or 'salt-cellar'. The circumference of the neck itself should be over the Adam's apple if this is visible, as it certainly is in most men.

In the accompanying diagram all those measurements that encircle the body, legs, arms or neck, are marked with a solid red line; those that measure from point to point are indicated by a dotted red line.

Unless you are coping with some very complicated garment, it is easier to take your measurements and draw straight on to the lining material. When this has been done and each measurement checked carefully, cut it out and see if it looks reasonable, then try it against a body to make sure before cutting into the real material. It is always easier to have a real person with roughly the same sort of measurements than a dummy which is armless and probably quite the wrong shape.

None of the patterns in this book calls for any particular skill in tailoring. The essential is to think of everything as a problem in arithmetic or architecture. Each diagram given has already been considered as a scale drawing. These have been carefully worked out and made up with excellent effects. As such diagrams can be misunderstood it should be noted that the scale is clearly marked at the bottom of each page: this is either 2 in. to each small square or 1 in. to a small square, depending on the available space on the page.

Wherever possible, fabrics of 36 in. or 48 in. have been used (e.g. pages 17-19, the three different uses of a half circle). Where such fabrics are not complete in their width for the whole garment, one seam straight across the fabric is better than two downwards, in which case selvedges should be sewn together. In the same diagram I have suggested the use of a smaller length of material for the extra addition.

Red has been used to show the outlines of the garment concerned; solid red indicates either the inside of the fabric or a lining or, in the case of the diagram on p. 25 an alternative use of the same pattern, cut down. Dotted red lines also indicate alternatives, but have a linking figure with the diagrams.

Measurements are only average, and must naturally be adjusted to the individuals concerned. Roughly I have made most of the men over 6 ft. tall and most of the women about 5 ft. 6 in.

As long as fabrics are cut in the manner suggested the economy is self-evident. The problems likely to prove difficult are those which arise from the use of one-sided materials (such as velvet) and patterned ones, where the design might appear upside down. To avoid the latter, only patterns that are obviously reversible should be chosen It is fatal to work in velvets from these diagrams without taking into account the difference in the pile when it is reversed. Parti-coloured garments are immediately more effective and simple in the two designs on page 25. Just watch to see which sides will fit before cutting out two left sides. Quite a useful exercise here would be to draw the diagram on a small piece of paper which has one coloured side, cut it out and make certain, if you have your front-right and your back-left cut, that you reverse the diagonal when cutting the front-left and the back-right.

Parti-coloured garments made their debut as fashionable extravagances, but in reality showed an amazing economy in an age when it was difficult to obtain the same dye twice. This difficulty still exists in many countries. Thai silk dyes, for instance, can still never be repeated; therefore it is better to have a complete contrast than a bad match.

The importance of linings cannot be stressed too much, especially in these

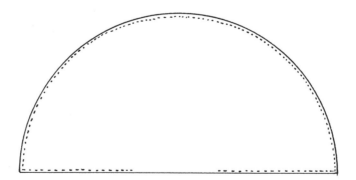

18. Method of lining half-circle which can conveniently be turned inside out leaving no edges to fray.

medieval garments, because their strange fullness must be obtained from circles and half circles, and whenever such shapes are used the inside must show on occasion, if not all the time. The usefulness of linings should also in some cases make a garment reversible as well as making it much easier to unpick or alter without fear of fraying.

It is best, in all cases, to cut out the lining exactly the same as the real garment. Place the two pieces together with the right sides facing each other and tack carefully all round the outside with the exception of the most convenient (possibly selvedge) side left open in order to turn it inside out. In this case 'inside out' means back to the right side of the fabric once more. When the tacking is satisfactory, and it is obvious that the two sides really do fit together and one is not stretched more than the other, machine the two pieces together over the tackings, turn inside out again and press carefully so that the edge is quite even and the seam right on the edge. At this stage it is wisest to hang the half circle, or whatever it is, over a rack or rail and leave the unsewn side to find its own level as much as is possible. You may possibly find that one of the fabrics has dropped overnight, in which case a due allowance must be made before doing up the final side.

19. Circular and semi-circular cloaks worn by ordinary people.

If the garment goes on stretching, it is best to run a tacking thread around the half circle some 4 in. from the edge. This will effectively stop the lining from hanging down over the edge but will not seriously interfere with the general effect. Very stretchy materials should be avoided. Do not attempt to line a really heavy material with a flimsy one. If each section of a garment is made in this manner there is no possible chance of edges coming unravelled or of seams splitting. All seams are firmer because the material is already finished and 'boxed' where it has been cut; the garment has twice the resistance to wear and tear of one that has not been lined in this manner.

Moreover, there should be no further problem of finishing off, no hems to be turned up, no necklines to fiddle with. The garment is in fact practically finished as soon as the linings have been installed and the main seams—if any —completed. Exceptional fabrics that are naturally double-sided, e.g. one side red and the other blue, can often be used for lighter garments with brilliant effect. A rayon jersey, for instance, often an amazingly cheap buy, can make a really marvellous garment if you should need dagging on the hanging sleeves, for with such a material there is virtually no need to make a hem at all.

The weave of a double-sided jersey normally makes the edges so firm that they do not fray, at least for some considerable time. Dagging can make a really magnificent effect if the character should need something extravagant in design, but it is a very tedious method of making an effect if you are pressed for time. Each leaf or scallop has to be carefully snipped on the inside before it is possible to turn it inside out effectively, often the lining is a looser material than the main garment, the pressing involved is a bit wearing, and in order to make certain that the two fabrics really are edge to edge it is often necessary to tack all round the scallops before pressing.

Wherever a lined garment is to be used make certain that the two fabrics are compatible, ensuring this by carefully tacking the lining to avoid stretching before it comes near the sewing machine.

CHAPTER 3

Religious Drama

The Costume for religious drama originally included the copes, dalmatics, chasubles and albs that belonged to the Christian Church. This is still one of the most effective methods of production because the actors taking part are endowed with the weight of Church apparel and to a great extent both their movements and thoughts are governed by what they wear.

It is an interesting exercise to try on a real cope, dalmatic and alb. The weight of the dalmatic and cope together make it impossible for the wearer to stoop. The shoulders are held back, the rising centre of the straight material at the back of the neck comes up almost to the ears restricting the neck movements, and adding much to the dignity of the stance. The long flowing lines of the loose cope in front swing slowly with each step, the trailing curve of the half circle at the back drags out, performing the function of a train. The line from the back of the neck to the ground has a beauty seldom seen in any other garment. The wearer has donned the garments of religious ritual. The bishop's mitre and the Pope's three-crowned mitre are both designed with the same purpose, even to the lappets that hang down behind.

Nearly all actors representing heavenly beings, saints, angels and other holy people originally wore some sort of ecclesiastical costume, and there are hundreds of paintings and illuminated manuscripts which show that the convention was a general one, though there are fascinating exceptions. The angelic host, from the Archangel Gabriel to the smallest and most insignificant little angel, wore, according to his degree, the cope, dalmatic or a simple alb, always with wings attached, sometimes miraculously, to their shoulder-blades. Some of the artists make these wings look as if they were strapped on over the alb; in other paintings they appear through slits in the copes, but such vandalism could not have been usual as the ecclesiastical vestments were all practically priceless because of the amount of fine embroidery that had been lavished on them. The appearance of 'slits' in these garments in a painting was entirely artist's licence. Ecclesiastical robes were invariably used in the church when

20. Angel wearing embroidered alb and girdle, wings apparently
attached with crossed-over stole. Damask cope with pomegranate
design and wings with peacock feathers.

religious plays were performed and the actors were thereby endowed with the magic of the Church.

Those actors who took the parts of ordinary people wore their ordinary clothes. Those who played devils had costumes devised for them whose origin lay in the most primitive forms of wild man's dress, comparable with the devil-dancers of any pagan community. They wore masks designed to create a sense of awe, more animal than human, with huge prominent teeth or tusks; their bodies were covered with fur or some shaggy material, often embellished with other hideous faces on various parts of their anatomy. Claws and hooves disguised their hands and feet and they were armed with whips, forks, chains or clubs in just the same way as a witch-doctor in any primitive society.

Many of the plays give delightfully detailed instructions for the actor and his costume. Perhaps the earliest of these was *The Mystery of Adam*, prepared for an Anglo-Norman audience in the 12th century. There are minute directions to indicate how this play is to be carried out.

Paradise is to be erected upon an eminence, probably built out from the top step of the church, so that God's dwelling is within the Church. It is to be surrounded by curtains and silk hangings to such a height that the people who are in Paradise may be seen only from the upper arm upwards. Sweet-smelling flowers and foliage are to be strewn about; in Paradise are to be various trees and fruit hanging from them, so that a place of delight may be seen. At the foot of the steps or eminence is the acting place where Adam and Eve go after the fall and where the scenes involving Cain and Abel take place. It is from this level that the audience view the performance. Inferno or Hell, whence the devils come and where Satan has his home, is on the right or opposite the church door. Hell has gates and smoke issuing from them. Demons clamorously rejoice with much beating on cauldrons and other suitable ironware. Costume details specify that God is to wear a dalmatic (or cope, translation here is a little difficult), Adam a red tunic, and Eve a woman's white silk garment with a silken girdle and mantle. Adam is to be well instructed to reply when he must, and he is not to be 'over-much quick' or slow in his reply. Not only he but all persons are to be instructed to speak calmly and to make gestures suitable to the thing whereof they speak, and in rhythm. They are neither to add nor take away a syllable but to pronounce all of them strongly, and those things which are to be said must be said in proper order. Whoever shall name Paradise is to look at it and to indicate it with his hand.

Adam and Eve walk in Eden and enjoy it. Devils below point at fruit. A serpent, 'cunningly contrived', lurks in one of the fruit trees. After the fall Adam and Eve take off their silken garments and put on garments made from leaves stitched together (fig leaves). Devils now sing 'Adam is made one of us'.

21. Devil wearing friar's robe and claw feet, other devil with mask,
bat-wings and claws.

Adam is given a digger and Eve a hoe and they begin to till the land; the devil is to come and plant nettles and thorns and thistles. Adam and Eve are stricken with violent grief and cast themselves to the ground. Then shall the devil come and with him several other devils bearing with them chains and iron fetters which they put round the necks of Adam and Eve. There shall be other devils nearer Hell who execute amongst themselves a pagan dance rejoicing at their perdition, and other isolated devils shall point them out as they are dragged into Hell's mouth, and they shall make great smoke pour forth as they shout amongst themselves rejoicing in Hell and they shall strike together cauldrons and metal vessels so that they may be heard outside. When a little while has passed devils shall go running about the place but some shall remain in Hell.

Then come Cain clad in red and Abel in white, and they also till the land. They make offerings unto the Lord and these are laid upon big stones which have already been made ready for them. The one stone shall be afar from the other, so that when God appears Abel's stone may be on His right and Cain's stone on His left. Abel is to offer a lamb, from which he is to make smoke arise. Cain shall offer a handful of grain. Also the figure of God appears to bless Abel's sacrifice and to despise that of Cain. Then Cain is to show a savage face towards Abel, and having made their offerings they shall go to their dwellings. Cain is then to come to Abel, wishing to entice him forth, cunningly, so that he may kill him.

In *The Presentation of the Virgin*, as played at Avignon in the 14th century, there are even more detailed directions for the actors and for the general staging within the church. Costumes are described variously, and the arrangement of the seats for the performers is explicit down to the cushion for Mary's seat so that she shall not appear dwarfed by her parents sitting higher than she is on either side.

A rough translation from the original directions reads as follows. One stage was to be erected in the middle of the church between the great west portal and the entrance to the choir, a little nearer to the choir so that it is clearly visible from all parts of the church. It was to stand 6 ft. high and to be 10 ft. from north to south in width, and 8 ft. from east to west. It was to be reached by stairways on the west and east, and such stairways should be 3 ft. wide closed by wooden boards so that nobody but the actors could use them. A railing 2 ft. high must surround the stage to prevent accidents and also to encase the actors. The floors of this stage, as well as the bench and seats upon it, must be covered with tapestries or cloth and the entire structure was to be built as strongly as possible to resist the pressure of the people.

A bench must be placed for Jacob, Mary and Anna on the north side extending from west to east, and so that the child Mary might be visible to the audience, her seat between her parents must be raised. Between the bench and the north side of the stage there must be space in either corner for the angels Gabriel and Raphael to stand beside and behind the Virgin Mary.

On the south side, two seats as high as the bench opposite must be occupied by Ecclesia and Synagoga, one to the east and one to the west. Two musicians were to stand in the corners of the stage behind these figures, their purpose being to balance the figures of Gabriel and Raphael (probably carrying trumpets).

Another smaller and higher stage was also to be erected between the choir stalls and the great altar on the northern side of the church. This stage was to be between 7 and 8 ft. high and 6 ft. square and also surrounded by a railing, this time only 1 ft. in height. It was to be carpeted with tapestries and equipped with a footstool and two cushions, one smaller than the other, both covered with silk and placed in the centre of the stage for Mary to kneel and sit upon.

Behaviour, music and the ordering of processions are directed with all the details necessary for the ordering of actors and the exits and entrances, right down to hand-movements. There are to be curtained dressing-rooms and a guard armed with rods to protect the actors from the press of the people, 'a guard of strong young men armed with spears'. The audience were instructed to follow the actors when bowing to Mary.

The details concerning the costuming of the actors and the properties are particularly interesting because they not only give directions but also supply us with pictorial details of medieval splendour and colours.

Mary's kirtle is to be white without any superfluous artifice, though it must be pleated. This probably means that it was to hang in the deep folds of a flared gown peculiar to the 14th century. Her mantle (cloak) too is white of 'sendal' or heavy silk. She wears only white and gold, symbols of purity and divine love.

Ecclesia is dressed with the most splendour. 'He is dressed completely in a Deacon's habit of gold, with a most beautiful embroidery, woman's hair (a wig?) spread out over his shoulders, and on his head he wears a certain golden crown with lilies and precious stones.' He carries a golden cross in one hand and a golden apple in the other, and wears a gilded calix attached to his breast.

Synagoga is dressed in dark colours and carries a ruby-red banner with S.P.Q.R. inscribed upon it.

Lucifer, with horns and huge teeth and a hideous mask drags chains, bright iron chains, by which he is bound to the Archangel Michael who must be armed in fair fashion and brandish a flashing sword.

Such directions give an insight into the emotional and stirring quality of medieval drama. Music, colour and action combined with a ritual quality of dignity, and the necessary awe that the church building was to impose, gave the audience a strong sense of religious participation.

Although these directions and many others exist, it is not until the early 16th century that we find a complete pictorial record of the costume changes that took place in a religious festival. Valenciennes staged a series of plays taken from the New Testament in much the same manner as the cycles in England; typical of the general trend of the time, but with one magnificent difference, the whole sequence was illustrated by Hubert Cailleu who also took part in the proceedings so that there is more than an element of truth in his pictures. The Valenciennes MS. was completed in 1547, some 40 years after the events recorded. Fortunately there are in the Bibliothèque Nationale in Paris two copies of the manuscript, beautifully illustrated in colour, with a complete list of the names of all the actors and actresses who took part. The illustrations give a real understanding of what theatre costume should be, and the characters are identifiable by the clothes they wear—the Orientals, the Hebrews and the Roman soldiers are all quite recognisable. Kings, Queens and potentates wear something approaching the styles of robe peculiar to their position, yet basically their costumes are simple, colourful and must have been possible to execute with considerable ease. What makes them doubly interesting is the fact that when on different days an actor would have to take different parts, his or her costume was not entirely changed but some delightful addition or subtraction was made to indicate the obvious change (see frontispiece).

The whole manuscript is full of unexpected and exciting details for anyone wanting first-hand information on how such plays were performed when they were originally staged. It would be difficult to find a more comprehensive example, and it is highly probable that the same or similar practices were followed wherever such performances took place.

From this point of view, it is a little sad for posterity that the Reformation in England changed the whole scheme of religious instruction, and there is nothing comparable in this country similarly recorded with illustrations. For although the 16th century is well documented from most scholarly standpoints, the religious problems of the age hindered freedom of thought and certainly the theatre suffered.

If we compare the earlier English writers with their understanding of Christianity we find that Chaucer's conception of the Friar was not peculiarly English, for the Devil who performs the tempting of Christ in the Valenciennes MS is portrayed disguised as a Friar; his hood only half on because of the horns that surmount his tonsured head, but there are bird's feet appearing beneath his gown, no doubt a much easier theatrical disguise than the traditional cloven hoof, yet giving that strange quality which bubbles up from the ancient pagan world and lends emphasis to the thought that devils are less than human and must carry the burden of their primitive origin. The producer was not apparently debarred from an expression of satirical humour at the expense of the Church, and his portrayal of this wolf in sheep's clothing is a characteristic contemporary skit of his own age.

This brief outline of the evidence that theatre costume was worn during the Middle Ages gives us something to work from, but there are still a hundred questions to be asked and answered about the easiest way to dress a medieval religious drama. Let us assume, first of all, that the ancient manner still has a very definite appeal. It is difficult to find the lists of garments that were worn and by whom, for what particular function or feast, what varieties of colour were used, and a dozen such tiresome questions the answers to which cannot at once be found in any encyclopedia. For those who wish to seek inspiration in such orthodoxy there are a number of points that may be helpful.

Ecclesiastical garments worn during the Middle Ages did not change very much after the 12th century. The three following centuries are those when religious drama was most popular and, although it continued in other countries well after the Reformation in England, its original form did not appear to change at all.

About the only general rule that could be applied to the wearing of the Christian vestments was that of precedence. The actor playing the part of God must wear the richest cope possible; a three-crowned mitre *glorifies* His head whenever He appears in medieval paintings. He is the head of the Church, and as the Pope appears wearing his full pontificals in order to impress so must God. Saints wear variously dalmatics, chasubles, and in some instances copes. So do angels if they are playing major parts. The Virgin often wears a cope also. It was the sense of endowment that provoked such a formula.

Colour also had certain meanings, and although these appear to refer to feast days and mourning they also signify other qualities such as rejoicing and purity, and were sometimes associated with the qualities of saintly people. It is impossible to insist that any one colour signifies any one quality, but the following lists may make it possible to rule out certain colours as being unsuitable:

LITURGICAL COLOURS

White. Trinity. Light, glory, innocence, purity and joy.
Black. Good Friday. Universal emblem of mourning.
Red.   Martyrs. Fire and blood, burning chastity.
Green. God's bounty; hope of life eternal (the spring of plants and trees).
Violet. Affliction and melancholy. The gloomy cast of the mortified.
Blue.   Mass of the Immaculate Conception. Hope.
Rose.   *Lætare* and *gaudete* Sundays.

Blue and green are the colours used for church decoration on ordinary Sundays, and blue also for all weekdays after Trinity. Violet, brown and grey for Advent and Lent. Violet stands for penitence, grey for tribulation.

The colours used by the different monastic orders should be known, and they are often hard to find:

Benedictine Black.
Dominican Black cloak over a white robe.
Carmelite Brown and white. (But in Pietro's Lorenzetti's paintings in Siena they are wearing robes horizontally striped in two shades of grey.) (See below.)
Carthusian White.
Franciscan Brown.

22. Carmelite monk as illustrated by Pietro Lorenzetti.

The details of Christian ritual garments or vestments are as follows.

Alb. The white tunic or long gown of linen worn by everyone who took his place in the choir. It was cut almost straight, having long sleeves and a straight opening at the neck (see page 42). Some of the albs worn by the more important priests, bishops and others were decorated with patches and bands of embroideries at the hem and also on the sleeves. It was the undergarment for those who wore the other vestments, but the sole visible one worn by the choir.

Amice. Several different definitions appear in contemporary writings but probably the obvious interpretation is that at some time it was a white linen cloth worn round the neck and tucked into the neck of the alb to protect the more important vestments from contact with the body. It was often furnished with an 'apparel' (embroidered decoration), and in many paintings is seen resembling an embroidered collar.

The *Almuce* is also described as a fur-lined tippet and hood worn by canons of cathedrals. This may refer to cardinals' hoods of the Middle Ages as well.

Chasuble. Originally a full three-quarter circle of rich fabric, sometimes only a half-circle; the Latin derivation is from *casa* or 'little house' (tent). This was worn at the celebration of mass and its colour might be changed according to the days the celebration took place (see opposite). The chasuble fell in graceful folds, as all such circular and semi-circular garments do, to well below the knees. So that the hands could be free to administer the sacrament, the sides were eventually cut away. During the Middle Ages the ritualistic movement of lifting the hands during mass made the sides fall back and revealed the contrasting lining. The effect was both beautiful and dignified, but presumably it did hamper the clergy who were not particularly aware of their robes. As late as the effigies in Henry VII's chapel in Westminster Abbey, we can still see the three-quarter circle, so it would seem that such robes were worn throughout the period. The chasuble was furnished with fine embroideries and orfreys, the latter covering the seams down the front and usually forming a cross from shoulders to the centre of the chest.

Dalmatic. Originally shaped like a cross and worn without any seams, it was put over the head and had a horizontal slit for the neck opening. The arm covering hung loosely over the arm and showed its lining when the wearer lifted his arms. There are several small changes in this garment, though it remains basically the same. Sometimes the sides and sleeves are joined up, sometimes the sides are left open and the sleeve only joined; again, sometimes flares or extra small pieces have been put into the sides to give it more movement. The decorations are rich and varied however it is worn. A curtailed edition was adopted by sub-deacons and called a *tunicle*. Normally the dalmatic was worn only by the Pope, bishops and deacons. Priests were not usually permitted to wear the dalmatic under the chasuble. During the 15th century the dalmatic makes a new appearance as a flared gown. This is to be seen in contemporary sculpture (see page 52) but was presumably one of the many excesses of the Church at that time.

Cope. A complete semi-circle of richly decorated fabric worn fastened across the chest with a great clasp. The copes of the Middle Ages were of superb workmanship, their embroideries executed by dedicated people, and the designs usually worked out with infinite care so that at no angle were they less gorgeous than at another. The real beauty of a cope is in its simplicity of cut. Probably no other garment devised by man could express so much dignity. The wearer must, however, be the correct height so that the hem at the back does touch the ground and not flap around his ankles. At the back of the cope hangs the 'hood'.

23. Pope with three-crowned mitre and hood wearing damask
cope with pineapple design. Bishop in chasuble and dalmatic
carrying a crosier of ivory and ebony.

24. Unorthodox robes worn in the 15th-century. On the left, a circular dalmatic worn with hanging sleeves and a collar. Centre, a cardinal's robe with deep cape and hood. Right, a square-necked, semi-circular dalmatic fringed at hem and side openings.

25. Cardinal in circular scarlet robe with slits for the arms. Hood lined with fur. The hat should have cords with five tassels each side. Pope wears an embroidered cope, dalmatic and gloves with the ring outside.

The straight edge of the cope is normally decorated with a wide strip of embroideries entirely different from the rest of the cope itself. In the 15th century a deep fringe was often worn at the hem of the cope, and the vestments of that period were usually far richer than those of an earlier date.

The decoration of these copes varied considerably, and probably the best way to understand the variety of embroideries and designs is to visit the Victoria and Albert Museum where some half-dozen magnificent examples are on display. These are made from velvet and heavy silks, damasks and richly embroidered fine materials. They are decorated with almost anything that might have some significance to the Church itself. Beautifully arranged flights of angels, the crucifix, scenes from the life of Christ, saints and their symbols, heraldic angels carrying the arms of saints, architectural mansions and pinnacles, and a thousand other motifs that might have some connection with Christianity. Whatever the design chosen, if a theatre cope is to be made it is most profitable to select a really large design or some fabric with gold or silver.

Maniple. Worn over the left arm, a strip of linen about three feet long and considered as a eucharistic garment.

Girdle. A long knotted cord worn around the waist over the alb or over the gown of a monk or friar. Denotes self-restraint and continence.

Stole. This was originally a narrow strip of material with embroidered ends which was worn around the neck and hung down to below the knees. It was often made from coloured silk and very delicately decorated with gold or silver, and frequently carried a deep fringe at the ends. It was worn under the dalmatic and the two ends can be clearly seen in portraits of bishops. The deacon was only permitted to wear it over the left shoulder.

It is as well here to put down a few of the restrictions and rules which the clergy were expected to observe in their costume. That they did not all do so is amply clear in the contemporary writings of the times. The Lateran Council of 1215 laid down the principle that clerics must wear garments closed in front and free from extravagances in length. Friars and travelling clergy must wear long robes; it was unseemly for the lower limbs to be undraped. The wearing of sleeved copes was forbidden. No fastenings of any kind were permitted on church vestments, with the exception of the clasp on the cope. Priests were not normally permitted to wear the dalmatic under the chasuble; the wearing of all the garments together was reserved for bishops and the Pope.

Chaucer thus describes the Monk in his *Canterbury Tales*: 'I saw his sleves rounded at the hand with fur, and that the fynest in the land, and for to fastne his hood under his chyn he had of gold y-wrought a curious pyn; a love-knotte in the gretter ende ther was. . . . His bootes souple, his hors in gret estate. . . ,'

CHAPTER 4

Heraldry and Symbolism

There are many mysteries surrounding the symbolism which is so much a part of medieval art in any form, and particularly in the art of the theatre where characters are often entirely allegorical. To appreciate something of the use of such symbolism it is as well to look into the habits of the time, the age of chivalry and romance.

The scholars of the Middle Ages were endeavouring to introduce a new idea into a Christian community whose teaching had come almost exclusively from the Bible. This new idea was Romantic, based on the works of the ancients and coming from Rome in much the same way as did Romanesque architecture. It had, perforce, to be superimposed upon Christian principles; Chaucer and other poets of the Middle Ages have left us brilliant pictures based on the knotty problem of introducing the pagan gods and heroes into a Christian setting. Romantic invention then, became an established method of expression; symbolism and heraldry a means of attaching a recognisable label to both real and mythological characters.

To the medieval mind, which for the most part was illiterate, signs and pictures meant a great deal more than the written word. This was one of the reasons for church decoration such as stained glass and wall paintings. People were confronted by a picture which could be understood as long as it was not too obscure in its meaning, but identity of certain characters had to be established visually and some general scheme had to be followed so that figures of saints were not too confused, so that virtues and vices were obvious, and certain living or recently dead personages of exalted degree were not mistaken for saints or angels. All this required a certain amount of organised thought, and heraldry and emblematic devices quite naturally furnished the clue to identification. But a great many artists had their own ideas of what particular symbol or emblem most suited a certain character. Because of this form of 'artistic licence' we are confronted by records of differing symbols which have at some time been attached to the same identity.

ARMS OF CHRIST AS KING OF JUDEA

DOUBLE HEADED EAGLE

COCATRICE

KING DAVID'S HARP

ERMINE

VAIR

26. Fourteenth Century Charges

A perfect example of this practice occurs in one of the earliest manuscripts illustrating an *Armorial* of all Christendom. The original manuscript was written and illuminated in the true medieval tradition, when the artist's pleasure and interest blinded him to the fact that such a beautiful record was going to be accepted by many generations to come as a true guide to heraldic devices. This artist was Flemish, his name Geire, and little is known of him except that he finished his very lovely work in the year 1372. His general scheme is to mix the arms of established families and personages with those of other Christian characters who have (long before the introduction of heraldry) made some contribution to the history of Christianity. Thus we find the arms of Biblical characters recorded side by side with those taken from the tomb of the Black Prince, or other equally well-known contemporary heroes. Establishing some heraldic device to identify a character, either real or fictitious, was a prevalent exercise throughout Europe at this time.

For our purpose, this work is of considerable value because it gives us a really contemporary picture and makes it easy to attach a device to a non-existent character. For anyone wishing to search further for information of this sort, Geire's original manuscript is in the Royal Library in Brussels. A copy was made by M. Victor Bouton in 1881 which can be seen in the British Museum under the title *Wappenboeck ou Armorial*.

Such heraldic identification extended into religious representation, and the churches of the Middle Ages were decorated with a profusion of arms devised to identify saints and even Christ himself. There are still a great many ancient churches where examples may be seen. Particularly interesting is the ceiling of the choir at St. Albans Abbey where some thirty-two shields are displayed. Some of these are the arms of various Lancastrian dukes and foreign kings connected with the House of Lancaster, but there are also the usual saints and in the middle of the ceiling the arms of Christ as King of Judea. This particular device (see p. 56 top left) was also employed to represent any noble figure who had particularly noteworthy Christian qualities, such as Godfrey of Bouillon who represented one of the Christian Worthies or Heroes in the famous sets of 'The Nine Worthies'.

Before going further into the mysterious inventions of early heraldry, it may be helpful to enlarge on the real and unreal figures who were the Nine Worthies, for they give us a very good picture of the sort of symbolism with which we are concerned. They appear in Shakespeare's *Love's Labour's Lost*, where they represent something which is comically ancient even by 16th-century standards.

A French poet, Jacques de Longuyn, wrote a poem in the early years of the 14th century with the title of *Voeux du Paon*, or in English 'Vows of the Peacock'.

In it he tells how the deeds of his hero, Porus, were braver than those of the nine great heroes of ancient lore. He then identifies the heroes as three ancient pagan heroes, three Hebrews and three Christians. The ancients come from Greece and Rome and are Hector, Alexander and Julius Caesar; the Hebrews from the Old Testament are David, Joshua and Judas Maccabeus; the Christians are Charlemagne, Arthur and Godfrey of Bouillon. They were chosen particularly for their places in valorous chivalry, and were therefore perfectly harmonious in the age in which poetic romance gave them reality. The artists who were expected to represent them differed in their opinions as to which arms some of the legendary figures should bear. Alexander and Hector, for instance, are often mistaken for each other because the use of a seated lion—gold on a red ground—seems to have been employed at certain times for both. There is still some doubt which of these figures is represented in the famous tapestry of the Nine Heroes now at The Cloisters, Metropolitan Museum, New York. One of the figures is missing and there is some speculation whether this is Hector or Alexander. This particular series of tapestries was woven during the last few years of the 14th century when the stories of the Heroes or Worthies was of considerable topical interest.

Most frequently we find that Alexander carries a lion rampant, Hector the seated lion, Julius Caesar a double-headed eagle. David aptly is given a harp, Joshua a cockatrice though sometimes this is a dragon, and Judas Maccabeus an eagle or some unidentified bird with outstretched wings.

The Christian Heroes are normally easier to recognise. Arthur carries three crowns symbolising England, Scotland and Brittany. These are gold on an azure field. Charlemagne has a divided shield with half a double-headed eagle (Rome) on one side and the fleurs-de-lis of France on the other, signifying his kingdoms in Europe. Godfrey of Bouillon is usually represented in armour as a crusader, and as such he carries the cross on his shield. The manner in which this is represented differs, but normally it is identical with that used for Christ as King of Judea. It is not known which came first, the emblems carried by Saints and Heroes as identifying properties, or the heraldic devices with which some of them are equipped.

The laws of heraldry contribute greatly to an understanding of some part of the mystery, but the whole subject is vast and intricate. When heraldry was first introduced in the age of chivalry its purpose was to make clear the identity of some person or personages, a family or an individual whose arms could make him recognisable. Already, by the end of the 13th century the use of heraldry was general, and during the 14th the designs were works of considerable beauty. The rules of heraldry served to eliminate a haphazard form of design and established certain shapes and symbols which could be easily seen

FESS   BEND   CHEVRON

CROSS   CHIEF   PALE   SALTIRE

PILE   ORLE   CANTON   LOZENGE

RONDEL   PALY   BENDY   BARRY

27. Heraldic divisions of the field.

at a distance. The first step then was to ensure that clarity was never confused by ornament, and the limited use of colour had to be established basically for this purpose. Rules evolved governing the use of colour on metals; for example only one colour could be introduced on either gold or silver, and should other colours be required they must be introduced within certain prescribed borders.

There was a language of heraldry which took its vocabulary from a mixture of French and Latin and gradually became recognisable throughout Europe. It is still in use today, and it is almost impossible to describe heraldic figures or divisions or colours without at least a rough idea of the vocabulary. Metals, furs and a limited palette of five colours were prescribed, and after that a series of divisions which could legitimately be made on the shield, borders, bends and bars of various sorts, and eventually the series of heraldic beasts and motifs.

The College of Arms or Heralds College was established as late as 1483, when heraldry had become so confused and complicated that there arose a very real need for an establishment that could make rules and regulations regarding the taking up of armorial bearings. Research into the subject in earlier centuries therefore is not easy.

The existing manuscripts dealing with the 12th and 13th centuries are records in the British Museum, and were made at the time of Henry III, and the first three Edwards. The basic principle was extremely simple: a clear motif indicative of something chosen by the knight for his arms and coat of arms. The two terms are to be taken quite literally, arms meaning his shield, and coat of arms meaning the surcoat or tabard which he wore over his mail and which was embroidered or painted with the same motif. Such a motif was called a 'charge', and its background, or the surface on which it stood, was termed a 'field'. In its earliest form, before becoming complicated by marriage or the taking-in of a series of other family emblems, it was a clear picture of an heraldic figure or figures, or a simple division of the surface. The sub-divisions which later occupied the College of Arms were often extremely complex, but for our purpose the heraldic simplicity of the 14th century could not be bettered. It was essentially theatrical because its intention was dramatic and immediately recognisable. When we read of a 'blazon' this means the verbal description of arms. The 'blazon' describes the 'charge', and the 'field', its division and colours. The right side of the shield from the point of view of its bearer is termed dexter, and the left sinister.

Heraldic colours are termed tinctures, and were as follows:

Metals: or and argent (gold and silver).

Colours: gules, azure, vert, purpure, and sable (red, blue, green, purple and black). Should a motif be in a natural colour and not one of these it was said to be 'proper'.

Furs: In the earliest representations there were only two furs: ermine which was originally quite recognisable as the tufts of a fur tail and not as a solid black shape, and vair. Vair started off as a combined pattern of wavy and 'nebulee' in azure on a field argent. These divisions are indicated below. There are also degrees of ermine with different colours having different names.

> *Ermine*, sable on argent.
> *Ermines*, argent on sable.
> *Erminois*, sable on or.
> *Pean*, inverted ermine, sable ground and or spots.
> *Vair*, argent and azure.

Varying divisions of the field were introduced at a very early date, and as long as nobody else had thought of such a division it was quite a straightforward distinguishing colour combination. The simplest ones have been shown on page 59 and some of the more complex on this page, but for obvious reasons a great many have been omitted and should any reader wish to pursue the subject further both the sources available to him have been mentioned. Any other books on heraldry were printed after the 15th century and bear little resemblance to the original simplicity of the animals and symbols.

Animals and beasts were particularly decorative, the elongated and foliated

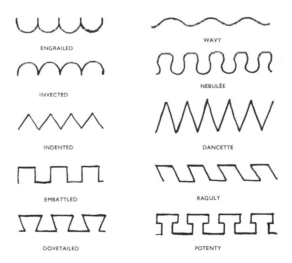

ENGRAILED

WAVY

INVECTED

NEBULÉE

INDENTED

DANCETTE

EMBATTLED

RAGULY

28. Heraldic divisions.

DOVETAILED

POTENTY

lion for instance, which probably was never intended to represent a realistic lion. He is frequently referred to as a leopard, and for the first two centuries of heraldry he continued to be a lean and elongated beast of great character. During the 15th century he began to look more like a lion, less long and with much more of a mane, his feathery fur took on a rounded appearance and at the same time the head became larger and less elegant. It was in the nature of designers during the 13th century to make figures long and unrealistic; a pattern was of more importance than realism in drawing.

Nearly all animals appearing in heraldic arms normally faced to dexter. The sinister side referred to bastardy and, although this was no particular reason for shame, the bar sinister indicated that its bearer was not the legitimate successor of his father, though he must have been accepted as his son. He could not carry his father's arms without the bar sinister.

This very sketchy outline of the simplest rules of heraldry should give a designer some help when confronted with the necessity of using arms of any

29. Synagogue from
    sculptured figure
    at Rochester.

sort. It is as well to consult the earliest books or manuscripts if particularly clear designs are required. Those recorded towards the end of the 15th century tend to be much more clumsy, realistic and over-decorated. It was an inevitable development at a time when so many families were engaged in establishing their own arms, or making impressive quarterings and divisions to show that they were related to the greatest in the land. A form which had been originally a simple visual identification became a complex status symbol. For theatrical purposes, the simpler the design the easier it is to understand, and wherever coats of arms are required in a medieval play it is as well to make these as clear as possible, eliminating any really fussy design and going back to the simple clarity of the 13th century.

The original directness of heraldry with its many limitations of colour and division, tinctures and charges, was a form of art that greatly appealed to many of the artists of the time. There are still existing manuscripts of the 13th and 14th centuries where not only arms, crests and helms appear as a form of decoration, but also the colours and symbols of heraldry are applied for illustrative purposes. For example, fur is indicated by the same definite and regular pattern used when 'ermine' or 'vair' is required on a blazon; and many illuminated manuscripts have a limited number of colours, the same azure, gules, vert and purpure with gold and silver leaf. Eventually the few recorded Royal Entries of pageants are decorated almost entirely with symbolic figures whose dress is inspired by the heraldic design of the city or guilds concerned. One of the best examples of this, though it is rather late, is the manuscript written and illuminated after the entry of Prince Charles of Spain* into Bruges in 1515; each figure is carefully described in the manuscript and the significance of the dress explained. Bruges herself appears a number of times, and such characters as Industry and Commerce are recognisable by the motifs which decorate their dress. Such a practice, if used today, could give an excellent sense of period to almost any formal production.

As for the more general use of emblems, most of these can be found in church decoration, because they represent Christian virtues. There is comparatively little else left to us of the symbolism of the Middle Ages that has escaped the ravages of five or six centuries.

Those who wish to use the emblems or attributes of saints would do well to consult a book on the subject. There are many hundreds of saints, and each of them is to be recognised by their 'attributes'. *Saints and Their Attributes* by Helen Roeder (Longmans) is a useful guide.

As far as the Virtues are concerned the problems of translation are bewildering, as well as 16th- and 17th-century changes which have become accepted as

* Royal Entry of Prince Charles of Spain. MS. in the Oesten-National Bibliothek, Vienna.

symbols now but were unknown during the 13th and 14th centuries. The following is a brief list of the usual symbols:

Mercy should carry a chalice signifying God's mercy to repentant sinners.

Peace usually carries the 'dove of peace', the dove sent out of the ark after the flood, who came back with the traditional olive branch in its beak. This sprig of olive is also used as a symbol by many artists.

Justice holds a sword in one hand and a pair of scales in the other.

Charity varies in her symbols more than her sisters. She is sometimes indicated with children, and sometimes with a dish of coins; it appears to be necessary for her to have some other figure to whom she is being charitable.

Truth carries a mirror.

Faith has either an anchor or a cross.

The allegorical figures representing respectively 'Church' or 'Synagogue' are subjects for surmise. According to the Catholic Encyclopedia, *Church* is crowned and sceptred, and carries a chalice in her hand emblematic of the supreme sacrifice and the sacrificial system. *Synagogue* is uncrowned, her staff is broken and her attitude betokens defeat, yet in the Avignon MS. of the Presentation of the Virgin she is described as carrying a banner and not a broken staff.

The problem of dressing allegory in some visually recognisable form cannot be so easily understood or defined, and no two artists ever agreed about which colour most suited the qualities of a symbolic or allegorical figure. One of the earliest of the allegorical paintings which may be regarded as giving a lead to future artists, was that of Ambrogio Lorenzetti, who in 1337–1339 carried out the decorations in the Sala dei Nove in the Palazzo Publico, Siena. In his *Allegory of Good Judgement* the figures which should interest us most as 14th-century conceptions are Peace, Fortitude, Prudence, Magnanimity (Charity?), Temperance and Justice. Concord is another interesting figure, and the little angels who represent Faith, Hope and Value.

Each of these figures carries a symbol. They are all crowned in some way, and there may be some special significance about the colouring of their garments. Concord wears a pink gown with beautiful golden embroideries, much the same as the angels wear in some of Giotto's paintings. She has a simple wreath, rather than a crown, decorated with precious stones; in her lap rests a concord, an instrument used in the Middle Ages and denoting harmonious agreement.

Peace is seated and leans on a cushion, which covers a suit of armour, her feet are placed on a shield. She wears a white gown with a tiny frill at the hem which resembles a Victorian nightgown. On her head is a wreath of olive leaves, and in her left hand an olive branch.

30. Peace with olive branch and Temperance with an hour-glass.

31. Fortitude
armed in Classic
manner.

Fortitude wears a black mantle over a black breastplate and shoulder-pieces in the Roman style; her right arm is shown wearing a red sleeve and in her right hand she holds a black sceptre with a gold knob on the top. In her left hand she holds a long shield. Her head is crowned with a golden, spiked crown (see above).

Prudence wears grey, and a white wimple with gold embroideries. Her crown is also gold, and fine gold and gemmed borders decorate both her robe and her mantle. It is difficult to see what the artist intended for the symbol she holds on her lap, but the words meaning both the past and the future are decipherable.

Magnanimity or Charity wears a dark crown which might have originally been of another colour, a blue gown and a white mantle over it; both are decorated with a black border. In her right hand she carries another crown which appears to be made of iron, in her lap a great bowl of coins which she holds with her left hand.

Temperance wears a pink gown and a pale blue mantle. Her crown is also dark but decorated with pearls. Her mantle is lined with gold. In her right hand she holds an hour-glass to which she points with her left. Amongst the entire assembly she is the only figure who wears her hair dressed in the style peculiar to the time with plaits doubled back from her chin to the sides of her head.

Justice is wearing a dull green gown with a black embroidered border, but her mantle is a Venetian red, not a scarlet, and lined with white. In her right hand she holds a sword, gruesomely balanced upon a decapitated head. In her left hand she also holds a crown almost identical with the one on her head.

Above these figures float little half-beings with their identity written beside them; these are Faith, Hope and Value. Faith carries a cross. Value, who is wearing all gold, appears to have a pineapple of gold in his hand. Hope is a vague, little winged figure all in pink with very pink wings.

While these are characteristic representations of symbolic figures in the mid-fourteenth century, it is impossible to make any definite rule as to the colours or the symbols which such figures should wear or carry. In *The Castle of Perseverance*, for instance, a play written about 1425, we find that the daughters of God are expected to dress in prescribed colours: 'The four daughters of God shall be clad in mantles; Mercy in white, Righteousness altogether in red, Truth in sad green, and Peace in black.'

About the only colours that we can safely prescribe for such characters are red for Justice and white for Mercy, but the predominance of these two colours, particularly in religious plays, gives us the impression that they were used to signify respectively blood and purity.

It should be remembered that though certain colours have been selected to represent certain characteristics this does not mean that such colours necessarily express the same emotions universally. In ancient Greece, yellow was a colour used to imply both cowardice and sensuality. It was chosen by the Church as the colour of Judas Iscariot's dress; yet for centuries it was also the royal colour for the state robes of Chinese Emperors. Perhaps yellow is the most difficult of all colours because of its confusion with gold. Gold of the sun, wealth and brilliance, yet yellow of jaundice and mud.

Green frequently expressed envy and jealousy, the colour of snakes and dragons, but was also the sign of youth and fertility.

Blue signifies all sorts of angelic attributes, and this is why we always see it as part of the Virgin's dress: chastity, loyalty, fidelity, piety and sincerity, as well as modesty, humility and divine contemplation. It was frequently used by artists for the robes of angels, as in the famous painting of Richard II in the Wilton diptych.

Purple, a royal colour for countless ages, is considered to express temperance in heraldry, and affliction and melancholy in church decoration.

Black again is a confusing colour, for though in *The Castle of Perseverance* it is used for peace, generally it is used for evil, falsehood or death. Heraldically it means wisdom and constancy.

At this point the reader may reasonably assume that there is no such thing as a plan to direct us in our search for colour-guidance in symbolism, and even that decision may be of some significance to the would-be designer!

CHAPTER 5

Hoods, Head-dress and Crowns:
Hose and Shoes

On pages 30 and 31 will be found diagrams suggesting how a hood can be cut from a limited amount of material. These are offered only as a simple method of making a hood and liripipe, but they do no exclude a dozen possibilities of making more complicated and perhaps more decorative and extravagant types of hood. There is no one single way of doing anything if time and economy are not essential. It would, however, be valuable for any wardrobe to own a set of hoods which could be used in several different ways; hoods in fact made to wear, as were those of the 14th century.

The hood in its earliest form was designed to give a maximum amount of protection to the head, ears, neck and shoulders. In some cases the shoulder-covering came right down to the elbows, protecting the chest and back as well as shoulders, which must always be most exposed to the weather. This part of the hood was called the gorget, although it was considerably larger than the armorial gorget. When the fashions of the 14th century began to demand the fancy edging of garments (known as dagging, etc.), all those with time and money to spare and a sense of fashion found the edge of the gorget a very suitable line for decoration.

Before the introduction of this fancy edging the liripipe, or lengthened point of the hood, furnished an amusing extravagance, though it was not an excess worn only by the wealthy. There are many contemporary illustrations that show the simple man working in the fields with a liripipe several feet in length tucked into his belt or even tied around his waist, with the head-covering hanging at the side. The extreme end of the liripipe was also used as a purse, no doubt a fairly safe place to store coins, and serving as a weight that might be used as a cosh in emergencies.

Hoods are a study in themselves, for they are so varied and rich in their arrangements that it would be impossible to reproduce all the styles which

32.   1. Hood worn over a hat. 2. Parti-coloured hood with front
split and turned back. 3. Monk with hood on shoulders. 4. Fur cap
with a knop on the top. 5. Hood with deep gorget. 6. Lined hood
with large face opening. 7. Cardinal's ermine-lined hood and
gorget. 8. Hood as worn by Chaucer. 9. Hat derived from the
wearing of hoods as hats.

have been suggested in the contemporary illustrations that we can still examine.
If we are to believe the artists of the 14th century it would seem that practically every man wore a hood of some sort; it was as necessary to him as the
coif and wimple were to his lady, and served as a neck protection when not
actually worn on the head. Often under the hood, or under a cap or helmet,
was worn a little coif like a bonnet; this was used primarily to protect both the
hair and ears, for during the 14th century long hair was worn by the majority
of young men. The general fashion seemed to be to cut it off somewhere below
the ears so that it was not too difficult to manage, though the youth of the time
took great pride in his really long hair which was often curled and 'pressed'

Chaucer's young squire, for instance:

> With him ther was his sone, a yong Squyer,
> A lover, and a lusty bacheler,
> With lokkes curled as if they lay in presse.

And the Pardoner of Rouncival:

> This pardoner had heer as yellow as wex,
> But smothe it hung, as doth a strike of flex;
> By ounces hunge his lokkes that he hadde,
> And therwith he his shuldres overspredde.
> Aul thinne it lay, in lengthes, one by one,
> And hood, for jolitee, wered he none,
> For it was trussed up in his wallet.
> He thought he rode al of the newe set,
> Disheveled, save his cappe, he rode al bare.

In the *Miller's Tale* young Absolem's hair was even more of an asset to his suit:

> Now ther was of that chirche a parisch clerk,
> The which that was i-cleped Absolon.
> Crulle was his heer, and as gold it schon,
> And strowted as a fan right large and brood.

Although it is evident that youths wore their hair long, the older man, who possibly was already beginning to get thin on top, preferred to keep his head covered.

Hoods then must be considered not only as a head-covering for warmth, but as a never ending source of head decoration; for when they were not employed purely for protection against wind and weather, they could be pushed back and worn as a shoulder cape or taken off the head and shoulders and hung safely by the long liripipe attached to some button or buckle on the gown. They were in fact often taken off and rolled into a hat, the face opening serving as the opening that was put on to the head.

A portrait of Chaucer himself wearing a plain hood (without a decorated gorget) shows that he too was familiar with this manner of head-dress, the gorget serving as some protection from draughts as well as being a decorative element (see page 70), but not completely covering the neck or shoulders. During the latter years of the 14th century this fashion led to the introduction of a majority of highly decorative hats designed from the idea of a hood with a dagged edge, but in reality being a complicated arrangement of a brim decorated with a semi-circular gorget and having an ornamental tippet hanging at the side, in much the same manner as had the liripipe when it was first used to tie around the head in order to keep the hood in the shape of a hat.

The conversion of the hood into the chaperon or hat was one of the most extraordinary of fashions. Presumably it first appeared when some wit was too hot in his hood and, not wishing to carry it, took it off and reversed the opening so that the dagged edge of the gorget arranged itself as a floppy, gigantic cockscomb which fell over his ears; in order to keep the gorget from being a nuisance to him, he then wound the liripipe around his head tying it in a knot to keep the whole fanciful erection within bounds. The effect is immediately amusing and curiously enough quite dignified, and again there is no end to the ways in which the gorget can be arranged.

Contemporary descriptions of dagging frequently use heraldic terms to illustrate the manner or shape into which the edges are cut. On page 59 and 61 will be seen just what such terms were intended to convey.

Again quoting from Chaucer, *The Parson's Tale*: '. . . endenting, or barrying, waving, palyng or bendyng, . . . and semblable wast of cloth in vanite.' Each of these terms refers to the traditional names of shapes or divisions in heraldry and as such are quite recognisable. The last two refer to the manner of dividing a parti-coloured garment (paly and bendy, see page 59).

On page 70 will be seen a parti-coloured hood. The top of the front has been left open, and turned back from the face, to display a contrast with the lining and to give some variety in the manner in which the hood is worn.

Clerical hoods and those worn by other dignified persons were often made with a much larger face opening so that they gave a bib or collar effect below the face (see page 70). This was often lined with fur and could be turned right back to form a collar or gorget, but there are many variations of this theme and it does not follow that every fur gorget was necessarily a part of a hood.

The hood of the fool or jester, who is so often termed Vice in medieval literature, is based on the same simple lines as that of the original useful hood, but in this instance the point or peak of the hood runs upwards rather than at a right angle to the face and forms a sugar-loaf shape if it were to be lifted up from the head. Sometimes this point is stuffed; sometimes there are two points rising from the head. Occasionally the peak is made in the form of a bird's head (see page 104).

The main difference lies in the fact that ears have been added to the sides of the hood, and often bells have been attached to the point or points. The fashion for bells to decorate the fine costumes of the time was introduced during the other excesses in fashion towards the end of the 14th century, and though to a great extent this was a courtly fantasy it remained the chief characteristic of the jester. 'The man of cap and bells' was for at least two centuries the court jester, and his costume remains a traditional example of a fashion which was at first peculiar to the 14th century.

It should be remembered that it is almost impossible to make a hood without a gorget, unless it is attached to a cloak or robe; there will always appear a gap at the back of the neck unless the line is carried down well over the shoulders, nor is it practical to try to join a collar to a hood. The original hood was intended to keep off draughts, as indeed were the majority of medieval clothes, and therefore vulnerable spots like the back of the neck had to be protected.

Comparable with the hood worn by all men, was the wimple or coif worn by practically all women at some time of the day. This charming head-covering unfortunately has never been sufficiently displayed in books of costume because of the competition of other fantastic and wonderful head-dresses worn by the ladies of the court during the 15th century. With such a wealth of fascinating information about the hennin and horns, butterfly, flowerpot and Oriental head-dress, the less exotic fashions have been rather overlooked. Such ornate styles were undoubtedly worn by the wealthy ladies of the time and the records of these apparently extraordinary edifices have had a widespread influence on theatre costume of all ages since. As early as the 1580's they were included in Bertelli's famous costume book, and as his works as well as Verchellio's have been an endless source for designers seeking inspiration, so has the hennin appeared over and over again in theatre design.

Inigo Jones introduced something of the sort in his Masque designs, and the very earliest books on historic costume gave them far more attention than their original use warranted. The less arresting head-dresses of the 14th and 15th centuries do not appear so often in print, yet their very simplicity and variety is amazingly useful for theatre design.

The wimple and gorget is probably the most attractive of all head-dresses for it makes a complete frame for the face. Its arrangement can be infinitely varied and there is no necessity for it to be one complete length of material. We have to bear in mind too that there are a great many materials made today which are by their very texture utterly unsuitable for this particular job. Originally wimples and gorgets were all made from fine linen, something in the nature of the softer cottons woven today; it is much easier to get the right sort of folds and drapes if a soft material is used—anything silky and slippery is to be avoided unless a great deal of time and dozens of stabilising pins are used. Do not attempt to imitate the formalised head-dress of the nuns as worn now, because theirs are head-dresses which were introduced when starch was in use; those which we need for the medieval plays were unstarched and as soft as possible.

On this page will be seen several arrangements that could be extremely effective and will put the wardrobe to very little trouble at all. The only necessary experimentation involved is to try out various ways in which such veils can be arranged to give the right sort of effect, and at the same time be comfortable. Always remember that the hair must not be seen around the face. Only brides (virgins) or unmarried women showed their hair and then it was usually held back from the face by a coronet or wreath even if it was to fall about their shoulders at the back. Curiously enough there never seems to be a painting of a young woman of that time who does not have curly hair, and in all the earlier romances the hair falls in even waves to well below the waist. Evidently curls were as fashionable then as straight hair and a fringe is today.

To save trouble with the arrangement of the wimple, it is as well to wear an elastic hair-band around the head, then if the wearer has a fringe this can be taken back under the band. This will also give a solid base on which to pin the

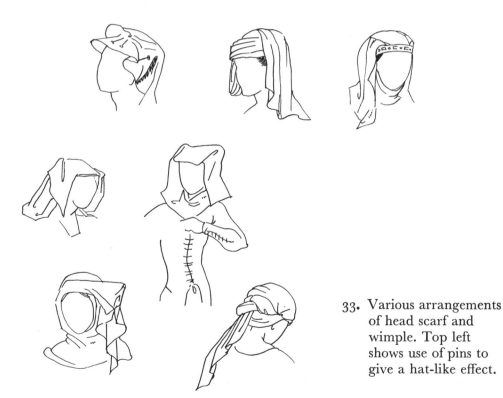

33. Various arrangements of head scarf and wimple. Top left shows use of pins to give a hat-like effect.

veil, apart from showing the purity of the forehead which was once considered the most beautiful part of a woman's face.

The simplest and quickest way of wearing such a head-dress is to pin one end of a piece of material (about one and a half yards long by three-quarters of a yard) to the top of the hair-band directly over the forehead, bring it down under the chin, over the top of the head again and leave one end loose hanging over the shoulder. Probably a discreet pin behind the ear will ensure that the loose end does not get too disarranged; such a pin should attach both the veil under the chin and the loose end to the head-band.

Several drawings of variations on this theme, as well as the more unusual arrangements of such a veil, appear in these pages. Experiment and a little ingenuity will work wonders for the individual concerned. We are in all probability experimenting in just the same way as our ancestors did when bored with a conventional idea.

The next most useful and simple style was that of wearing the hair plaited in shells over the ears, and decorating such a simple structure until it assumed quite fantastic dimensions. First we must assume that the plaited hair was covered with openwork, shell-like structures which were attached to a narrow

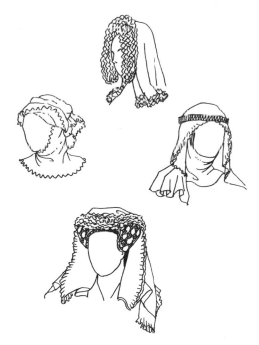

34. Goffered and decorated veils worn in various ways. Bottom figure shows the hair in shells over the ears.

coronet or head-band. The 'shells' were composed of fine metal wire, and where the wires crossed a bead or pearl was used to hold them in place. Such shells are very simple to make and can be used over and over again. It does not matter in the least if there is hair inside them or not. Any suitable silk lining can be used, and almost any sort of wire, though copper looks better. Over this simple structure a veil was worn; it could be perfectly plain or, as indicated on the last page, have several layers of goffered edges showing. The best effect can be obtained by using such things as ordinary shoulder-pads, sewn to a head-band. The decoration of these is not restricted, but the size and shape of the shell form can be anything from six inches to a foot high. It can be a complete round, or conical, or a triangle.

An earlier style (*c.* 1350), equally simple to imitate, is that of a coronet with wires attached at the sides to form bars on which the plaits are to be arranged. This is particularly effective for an actress who already owns long, straight hair and has sufficient time when dressing to arrange it beforehand without any rush. This is not advisable if there are only five minutes to spare, as the hair has to be bound in position on the framework. Again a small flimsy veil hould be worn over the top of the head. Normally only the edges of such head veils were decorated in any way, and there are several delightful little decorations to be studied that give the impression that seed pearls had been used as well as fine embroideries and frills, and something resembling a decoration like our modern ric-rac braid (see page 75).

Crowns and coronets are continually in use in any theatre wardrobe, and there are a number of rules about these. Tradition still governs the wearing of the ceremonial coronets by the nobility and, although a very great variety of designs were introduced in the Middle Ages, the present arrangement of strawberry leaves and balls appears at a very early date. Dukes' coronets have three balls between large strawberry leaves. A Marquis has a single ball which is considerably larger and well above smaller strawberry leaves. The coronet of an Earl carries single large balls and minute strawberry leaves in between. Kings and queens have been given more licence in their choice of decoration, and some of those that I have chosen to illustrate on the accompanying pages show a delightful freedom from convention; especially is this noticeable during the 14th century. The Madonna's crown on the opposite page, with its lovely flat foliation merging into the halo behind, is eminently suitable for theatre design.

The use of the fleurs-de-lys, trefoil or cross between pinnacles carrying some precious jewel or a pearl, seem to form the basis of the majority of designs, but there are also a great many that are purely scrolled, ribbed or scalloped. It was the necessity to decorate with jewels that inspired the designers with a particular interest in points and formalised leaf forms.

35. Crown worn by Richard II, tall crown worn by 14th century
King and foliated crown worn by the Virgin Mary.

It is as well not to try to make crowns from silver or gold foil. There is too much reflection from lights, and therefore too much attention called to such crowns. It would have been impossible to wear a solid gold crown at any time, the weight would have made this unbearable, and to examine any which are still to be seen in many museums is to find that they are more in the nature of filigree or gold wire, a fragile delicate mesh rather than a solid metal structure, their purpose rather to hold the jewels in place than to enable the wearer to be 'crowned with gold'.

The coronet and crown as worn today for ceremonial purposes is normally worn over a velvet cap, the velvet showing through the design of the gold. We first see something of the sort in the curious idea which seems to appear in many pictures, not necessarily portraits, of wearing a crown over a hat. This is a peculiarly 15th-century convention, but there are a few instances of it having been used earlier. The pictures which show this most often are those illustrating either classical mythology or such characters as the Magi, kings and princes in fiction or romance and also probably in theatre as well. It was certainly a very useful method of distinguishing a royal figure from his followers without the necessity of wearing a full crown over a bare head, obviously unsuitable even for a king if he were outdoors.

Royalty and ecclesiastics were not the only figures whose clothing and head-dress were characteristic, distinguishing features. There were a great many figures during the Middle Ages whose dress was intended to proclaim their status in society, and this was one of the many reasons for the endless succession of sumptuary laws prohibiting such-and-such a man from wearing certain types of clothes. These laws were seldom enforced, but the normal laws governing official wearing apparel were adhered to because they had become symbols of dignity rather than extravagances.

It was from this time that gowns became the identifying garb of doctors or men of learning, that Caps of Maintenance distinguished the man of law, that the hood worn hanging behind when the cap was in use first established the fashion for hoods worn by academics today. It is, however, extremely difficult to point to one figure painted during these years and say definitely that such-and-such a shape is a Cap of Maintenance of some particular date in such-and-such a country. The only possible course is to look at a variety of illustrations that we know were intended to represent counsellors, princes or doctors of various sorts; then make **our own** selection and judgement of what seems to represent the most obvious **or stage**-worthy design.

36. Three caps of Maintenance with ermine lining showing. Top left, Edward the Black Prince, Canterbury Cathedral; bottom left, Jan Gossaert's painting of *The Adoration*; that on the right is the hat worn by Agamemnon in the Tournai tapestry (V. & A. Museum) *Wars of Troy*.

37. Hoods and caps worn by the Counsellors in the Valenciennes MS. Note the general use of tabards and split tunics.

There is a bewildering amount of material from which to draw our conclusions, and in the accompanying pages I have endeavoured to illustrate various examples. In each case the source is given because rarely are counsellors, elders or doctors illustrated alone, and where there are groups of several there do appear to be certain differences in their costume and the manner in which they wear their caps or hats.

Written descriptions of various head-dresses are often too difficult to follow, but there are one or two that were set down during the 15th century that are enlightening. This quotation from the stage directions of *The Coventry Mysteries: The Council of the Jews to the Crucifixion* (Shakespeare Society's edition) is given here in modern English:

'Here shall Annas show himself in his stage, dressed as a bishop of the old order (Hebrew), in a scarlet gown and over that a blue tabard, furred with white, and a mitre on his head after the old law. Two doctors (or Counsellors) standing by him in furred hoods and carrying before them their staves of office, each of them wearing on their heads a furred cap with a great knob in the crown. Standing in front of them, dressed as a Saracen, is Annas's messenger.'

This particular description gives a fascinating insight into the careful thought for costume detail which was provided for the better understanding of the plays. The 'Old Law' is illustrated in the Valenciennes MS., wherever the ancient priests are concerned in that particular 'act'—they all wear a 'tabard'

over another garment, they all wear a 'Mitre' which often takes the form of
two overlapping crescents. In fact such a head-dress could quite well be a
Christian mitre put on sideways. The two doctors with their furred hoods
to indicate their official dignity (worn hanging down in front, revealing the
fur, see page 70) 'about their necks', their staffs of office very much in front
to indicate their dignity, and the most difficult of all things to interpret, their
hats—'furred caps and a great knob on the top'. A great knob on the top of
the Jewish hat was a common distinguishing mark of the wearer's position in
life during the Middle Ages. We can see several drawings of this strange knob
in most of the illustrated manuscripts, but they are all part of a hat, not a furred
cap. There is a great lack of information about such delicate details.

The endless query as to what some particular in clothing really meant
at any given time must necessarily defeat any historian. The vocabulary of the
Middle Ages was so different from that of a time when dictionaries had been
invented; the use of words, or the written word, being something that still was
an individual or entirely local term does confuse even today; how much more
difficult these terms are in this century when even the Bible (translated some
two or three hundred years after the times in which we are interested) has had
to be rewritten in order that it can be understood by a modern generation.

All hose were coloured, even those worn by women, and Chaucer remarks
upon the Wife of Bath's 'hosen of fyne scarlett red, ful streyt y-tyed, and shoes
ful moyste and newe'.

The long hose, or what we would now call tights, were not the elegant
ballet-tights of today. They were made from stretchy materials and cut on the
cross in just the same way as other figure-fitting garments of the time (see page
27). The effect of these, at least when worn by the poorer people, was much
the same as that of jeans, and an ankle-boot covered the instep and fitted over
the bottom of the long hose. There are a variety of leg and foot coverings to be
found in pictures of the time. Probably one of the easiest and simplest methods
of producing such an effect for the stage is to wear a thick black sock over the
hose and roll it down to the ankle. A sole can be sewn easily on to this, producing
much the same effect as the Italian slippers with a knitted upper on a canvas-
covered sole.

Curiously enough there seems to have been a theatrical convention,
judging from the Valenciennes MS., that 'boots' were worn by all characters
including women. These 'boots' do not appear to be anything more solid than
a sock, but it is possible that they were made from some very soft leather. Even
the figure of Salome wears boots half-way up her calf, and her dress is split to
the thigh. The peasant, as depicted in his own age, wears his home-made hose

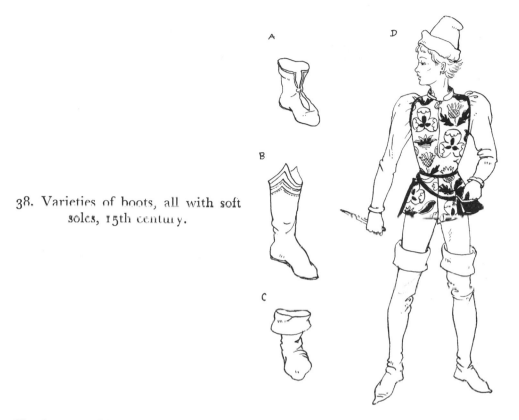

38. Varieties of boots, all with soft
soles, 15th century.

like long stockings which were tied to the belt at the waist, and not joined together at the trunk. The suggested diagram for making these garments can be followed with confidence; they do work and they produce the desired 'chunky' effect never to be achieved from the tights which are normally worn and are supplied by all theatrical costumiers. Materials such as hessian or woollen jersey should be used.

In contemporary pictures and tapestries of men working in the fields the lower leg may be seen encased in straw, similar to the straw covering of a wine bottle (see page 85), or the hose worn hanging down and the knees bare, or the ankle is bound with rope to hold a skin covering over the foot, or a dozen equally ingenious ideas to give some protection to the foot. William Langland in his *Creed of Piers Plowman* tells of the poor peasant with 'his hosen overhangen his hokshynes . . . al beslomered in fen'.

Footwear always becomes a mounting worry, and however skilled a wardrobe may be, it is unlikely that anyone can seriously undertake to make appropriate shoes that will last through any production. It is possible, however, to make felt coverings for such things as old tennis shoes or flat bedroom slippers, and it is quite a simple undertaking to turn these into boots if there is time to do so.

It is most important to see that everyone has flat-soled shoes. No heel at all was worn except on the wooden pattens, or 'cracows' as they were called. This flatness produces quite naturally a difference in walking, the same movement as sandals or bare feet, and the clothes of the Middle Ages with their sweeping hems cannot be managed unless the shoe or boot is both flat and fitting.

39. Cracows with wooden soles.

40. Peasant wearing coif and using his tabard to carry corn, etc.

Shoes were made from coloured leathers and the wealthy indulged their fancy not only in long 'piked' or pointed toes, but in brightly coloured footwear, often stamped with designs in gold or contrasting colours. Leather was not always used; velvet and other rich and brilliant materials were employed and cloth of gold could be used by noblemen. The cutting-out of intricate designs and the 'tooling' of the leathers gave to the shoe an ornamental interest seldom achieved at a later date.

The general method of fastening the shoe was by a lacing on the outside of the foot, but the flimsier and more elegant shoes of the early part of the century were often fastened in front. Cutting the edge of all garments into leaf shapes or points was a fashion that found its way on to the upper edge of boot or shoe.

The 15th century was a century of excesses, and shoes were one of the most extravagant absurdities of the time. The wealthy were struggling hard to maintain their *status quo*, and tried with diminishing success to bar the rising middle classes from interfering with their prerogatives in fashionable absurdities. In the year 1420, a law was passed barring the wearing of long 'piked' shoes by any person whose income did not exceed £40 per annum. A prince, however, might be permitted to wear his 'pikes' two and a half feet long if he wished. It is not advisable in the theatre to indulge in the elongated pointed shoes peculiar to the age, unless they are especially valuable to a particular character.

One of the practices of the time, most useful for theatre purposes, was that the hose were often 'soled' and the general effect in so many paintings of the Middle Ages is that no shoes are apparently being worn at all, and the ankles of the hose are laced up on the inside.

CHAPTER 6

Properties, Armour, Masks and Wings

There are a bewildering variety of properties associated with medieval drama, and few can be borrowed or hired. The strangely beautiful shapes natural to the Middle Ages can give a significant and lovely finish to a production, but hardly any of the vessels and other everyday objects which were used then exist now, even in museums. This makes it particularly difficult for the property-makers to find suitable examples from which to take their designs.

The properties mentioned here are only those which have to be carried as part of the dress of certain types or characters. For instance, a musician must carry some musical instrument, a fool his bauble, a knight his sword, and so on. It is the actual proportion of such objects that it is necessary to appreciate, rather than the delicate details of their workmanship.

Certain small properties should also be understood, though their illustration is not necessary. Courtiers serving at table should carry a towel over their shoulders and this, as can be seen in many of the manuscripts, is not similar to our table napkins today: it usually has a bordered edge and sometimes even a fringe at the ends. It is white and appears even in the pictures of feasts outdoors.

Peasant women are rarely empty-handed; the distaff seems to have been perpetually in their hands. People working in the fields would carry an assortment of gear, and often a collection of knives and small packages pinned to their tucked-up skirts, or even a sort of pad on one hip purposely designed to make their particular job easier or to help in carrying a heavy basket or other load (see opposite page).

Pouches and pockets were worn by everyone. Such pockets were in the nature of a handbag and were hung from the waist of the women; in some cases under the skirt or apron, but sometimes showing.

Property-making is an art which deserves more attention than it generally gets. This does not mean that a lot of time should be lavished on insignificant detail, but it is important that the silhouette should look convincing and the

41. Properties for sheepherds. Pads on hips and coarse leg coverings tied at knee and ankle.

actual proportions, compared with the human frame, should be right. For instance, a bishop's crosier looks far more impressive if it is made on a grander scale. Anything less in size than the example on page 87 could appear more like the crook associated with 'Little Bo Peep' or an 18th-century pastoral of nymphs and shepherds.

The last thing one wishes to do in religious drama is to make it absurd by excessive disproportions, but often with the very best intentions this happens solely for lack of appreciation of this problem of comparative sizes. Grandeur must have size, and such size when connected with theatre should be exaggerated. Practically all rich properties should give a sense of weight, because they were in all probability made from heavy materials so that they would last as well as be impressive. Crosiers of heavily gilded silver, solid ivory, or ebony were all ponderously weighty to carry and helped greatly to ensure the slowness of movement required in Church ritual and processions. The little model of a church which sometimes appears just below the crook itself was usually a thing of great beauty, and often made of gold and jewels. This was the symbol of the Church and decorated the crosiers of the Middle Ages. The fact of having such a weighty decoration made it necessary to hold the crosier as near to the weight as possible.

The gifts of the Magi should also be impressively weighty; they were the rich gifts of kings and were of gold and silver studded with gems. If a cardboard box is decorated to give such an impression it should be weighted; it is immediately incongruous if it is waved about with the ease of its actual weight. Probably during the Middle Ages the church plate was often used for this particular performance, but modern church plate is too small for such a purpose, and bears little resemblance to the designs of the Middle Ages, even if it could be borrowed for the occasion.

Exaggeration of size applies also to such appendages as angels' wings, especially if a performance in a church is contemplated. Angels must not look like a fairy chorus, their wings should be as large as the space available permits; and they should tower above the heads of the wearers and give the impression that they are large enough to support the figure to which they are attached. If Satan wears chains, they must be heavy clanking chains; if St. Michael or the Angel Gabriel carries a sword, see that it is an impressive one designed in the fashion of the great swords of the 14th or 15th centuries—not a rapier of the 18th century.

Intentionally, properties have not been illustrated in these pages isolated from the figures which are to support them, because it is their size in relation to the individual actor which gives such things their correct significance. Even sceptres and orbs have a sort of standardised size, and on page 100 I have

42. Bishop with fringed cope carrying crosier with 'church' decoration. Mitre
joined at top.

introduced a figure to bring such details into scale.

Whenever armour is necessary we are faced with the very great difficulties of its manufacture, and although there are many ingenious ways in which theatre armour can be made, none of them can be undertaken lightly. To simulate plate armour, one needs first of all a body on which to mould the shapes of the various pieces. This is not easily come by, nor is it practical or economical to build up such a figure, or parts of a figure, in clay. The normal methods in theatre workshops are either to work with felt and glue, or a more up-to-date material, called Samco, which has to be moulded with acetone. Neither of these methods should be undertaken when there is a shortage of time or of skilled labour. It is also possible to work with some chance of success with chicken-wire and papier mâché, a form being made from the chicken-wire before the papier mâché is applied. When the surface is sufficiently solid-looking and quite dry, a layer of plaster of Paris or alabastine, or some other quick-drying surfacing, can be added and the whole painted, first black and then with paint simulating the colour and texture of steel.

It is far better, however, to work towards a general effect than to attempt to instruct unskilled workers in tricky mediums such as felt and glue, selastic and acetone. As mentioned earlier, armour can be hired and several theatrical costumiers specialise in it.

The general effect of armour does not appear so great a problem if we remember that during the Middle Ages armour was not worn without some sort of covering. Surcoats, tabards and jupons of various sorts were the natural protection for the breastplate and body-armour. These were worn in varying lengths from mid-thigh almost to the ankles. They were split either in the front or at the sides, and normally showed the legs and arms only. The sword and sword-belt of fine workmanship were worn over this covering and may be seen on most of the tombs that exist today as the most important part of the whole costume.

Chain mail was worn generally until the beginning of the 15th century, though it was often embellished with plate. For our purpose there are a great many materials that can give the impression of mail—and I do not include dish-cloths dipped in aluminium paint, though this particular device is still used by many of the hire firms. A loosely woven jersey material, preferably with a black base, having a silver thread woven through it, is obtainable in many shops. Its texture is light and this quality might seem to make it undesirable for the simulation of anything as heavy as chain mail. However, if it is lined with a fairly heavy material (preferably off-white to help catch certain lights and give a better texture), the illusion can be extremely effective. The 'chink' of mail can be imitated by attaching strings of small metal curtain rings

43. 14th century representations of angels; note size of wings.

to wrist or knee. Sleeves, leg-coverings with feet, and gorgets, can all be made in this way, and the addition of a helmet makes any figure so dressed very convincing. It is as well to pad under the tabard because a breastplate was always worn, and a sense of thickness is of the greatest importance for an armed figure. Nothing can be less impressive than a lightweight clinging tabard worn by a slim young man; he cannot look like a knight, least of all like one equipped for battle. The breastplate was purposely rounded away from the chest in order to protect the wearer from attacks nearest the heart. The rounding also acted as a slippery surface to divert both sword and arrow.

Swords, scabbards and sword-belts are often the greatest of the many stumbling blocks in the way of armoured actors, because frequently they are not seriously considered earlier than a dress rehearsal. They should rate among the most important properties which can make or mar a production. Swords cannot be worn just stuck into a leather belt; they must hang in a position where they are immediately at hand and yet not in the way of free movement.

The sword-belt is not just a leather belt to be worn around the waist. Its position must be absolutely correct for the actor concerned so that the scabbard moves with ease with the body, and does not either trip him up or get in any-one else's way. Belts, swords and scabbards should be ready at the first rehearsal. This will give the actors time to get used to a particularly difficult feature of their costume, and they will after one or two rehearsals be able automatically to adjust themselves and their swords to the conditions and restrictions of the acting area. They may even find that the sword can be a help to their acting instead of the all too obvious hindrance it so often appears in theatre productions.

A variety of drawings from various sources appear on the opposite page. A sword without a belt can be used only when a two-handed sword is needed, in which case it is normally carried by an esquire or a servant and handed to the knight when any action is expected of him.

A curious feature of much of the contemporary armour illustrated in the Middle Ages, particularly for romances and theatre, is that so much of it appears to be unrealistic. A figure-fitting breastplate, obviously inspired by the records of ancient Rome, is frequently coloured and makes no attempt to give an impression of metal; an instance can be seen in the frontispiece. This particular example is by no means unique, and there are several others in which the breastplate actually has creases in it. It seems possible that some kind of moulded felt was used for pageantry even during the 15th century, an extremely interesting convention which could be followed with equal success today, for it has the effect and something of the silhouette which makes theatre costume convincing. The passion for 'real' stage armour of the medieval period

44. Two knights and a bowman wearing tabards and tunics over their armour.

45. 14th century
representation
of classic armour.

was first used during the romantic revival at the beginning of the 19th century, no doubt inspired by the Ghost in Hamlet, and having something to do with the consuming interest then in the Gothic rather than the classical. It was used by Charles Kean in many of his productions during the mid-19th century, and appears to be dying a very slow death. Probably the realism of that time was inspired by archaeological research and the many books published illustrating tombs and brasses, but which had hitherto been isolated examples of the past. Whatever the cause, it had a lasting effect on theatre productions; there is no reason at all why some newer, or older, convention should not be equally or more effective.

The majority of the medieval plays were concerned with the historical interest in the life of Christ, and it appears from a variety of evidence that the actors playing the parts of Roman soldiers did wear something that made them look like Roman soldiers, not contemporary ones. The costume designers of the 16th century were also particularly interested in the type of Roman armour which followed the indentations and contours of a man's body, exaggerating his muscles and build so that he looked a better developed specimen than the man who was not a soldier. Amongst artists of the time there was apparently some division of thought as to whether an armed angel should wear classical or contemporary armour, so we are free to make our own choice.

Tapestries woven as early as the 14th century show an interest in armour of the past, as well as in that of their own time. In the set of tapestries already mentioned (page 58) depicting the Nine Heroes, one of the smaller figures standing to the left of the seated figure of Alexander is distinctly Roman in his style of armour. He wears a breastplate and helmet and a short-sleeved tunic, and his knees are bare. He is in every detail different from the other figures, who are definitely of the 14th century, except for the conception of a chain-mail gorget or collar.

Tapestries generally are some of the more interesting sources for research into theatre costume, not because they can be accepted as showing an actual performance as it took place during the Middle Ages, but because they mostly illustrate subjects from which such plays were taken; the romance and poetry of the age with which we are concerned, as well as the more exciting Biblical scenes and allegorical figures as they were depicted at a time when their existence was accepted. All of these beautiful crowded scenes give the most valuable information about costume details and properties, armour in particular, with far more delicacy than do most illuminated manuscripts.

In the late 15th century tapestries, such as the Tournai series in the Victoria and Albert Museum illustrating the *Wars of Troy*, is presented another type of decorative armour especially designed to convey the foliated and fantastic effects associated with such heroic figures. Such wealth of interesting and impractical workmanship is later to be seen in the masterpieces by the great masque designers of the 16th century, such as Primaticcio, Bountalenti and eventually Inigo Jones. Beautiful and fanciful as it is, suggestions for the making of such extravagant armour is beyond the scope of this book and beyond the capacity of most theatrical wardrobes.

The Court Jester or Buffoon, or Vice as he is often termed in the morality plays, carries his 'bauble' or doll on a stick. These are delightful excursions into fantasy, things of the ancient world bearing singular resemblances to primitive art. Evil faces in the style of Hieronymus Bosch predominate in the majority of medieval illustrations, probably fashioned from natural branches of wood with the gnarled end suggesting a head. They were touched up, painted and adorned to accentuate their likeness to a caricature of humanity. One such bauble is in the hand of 'Vice' in the Fouquet miniature of the martyrdom of St. Apollonia (see page 95). Another similar though much more finished bauble is to be seen in the series of tapestries depicting *Le Condemnation de Banquet* now in the Museum at Nancy (page 103). Sometimes such baubles were delicately fashioned portrait heads of the Buffoons themselves, complete with cap and bells, the puppet head being attached to a stick and not

46. Fanciful armour worn by Agamemnon in Tournai tapestry
The Wars of Troy.

necessarily part of the branch. A pig's bladder was also carried in this way, and a convention perpetuated today by the clown in circus and pantomime.

If masks and wigs are going to be made at all in the wardrobe, it is as well to see that they are not being made at the same time as costumes. Much better to find some outside place with a sink for the making of masks, and some quiet corner where nobody is likely to come pushing by while a wig is being made. Masks go through various messy stages from wet modelling-clay to the tiresome drying period, when they can be wrecked if moved or knocked over.

Masks can be exciting to make because the grotesque peculiarities of designs for devils or other fiendish beings can come to life with unexpected qualities. Inspiration for many magnificently devilish masks can come from the works of primitive artists, particularly from Africa, Java and Ancient Mexico. They should first be modelled in ordinary modelling-clay, or even plasticine. Measurements must be taken of the actor who is to wear them: the width of the eyes, the size of the nose, depth of chin and width of face, so that he can see, breathe and talk.

The clay (or plasticine) model must be covered carefully with vaseline

47. Vice as illustrated in Fouquet's *Martyrdom of St Apollonia*.

before applying papier mâché, of which several layers are needed. Each layer *must* be allowed to dry before the next is applied. There is a Dryad book of instructions on how to use this mixture of newspaper, paste and water. When the papier mâché is quite dry it should be surfaced or smoothed down (if necessary), and a layer of thin plaster painted on before the details of the face are painted in. The addition of feathers, straw, shavings or bits of fur can greatly enhance the general effect.

Another method is to use buckram instead of papier mâché. Buckram contains glue which enables it, when wetted, to be moulded to any shape over a modelled surface. These masks are similar in texture to the more expensive carnival masks that can be purchased at toy shops. Carnival masks can sometimes be used quite effectively if they are painted over, but normally their colouring is too brash to make them useful as they are.

When animal heads are required, a framework of chicken wire is the most satisfactory base. Hessian, plaster and paint are probably easier to use than papier mâché on a construction of this size. Wood-shavings, unwound ropes and the material used to stuff drain-pipes are all singularly useful in representing animal hair. If rope is used it should be combed out with a curry-comb, and this takes some time.

Realism is not a quality to attempt. It is much better to give an impression than a painstakingly exact replica of an animal. Always see that an animal head has a 'gorget' to cover the shoulders of the wearer, and it should be considerably larger than the head on which it is worn. As early as *The Mystery of Adam* the serpent had to be 'cunningly contrived' (see page 43), and such cunning contrivance should be the aim of anyone who undertakes to make masks. They are a personal business, and their ultimate success lies in the ingenuity of the maker.

Wigs need the undivided attention of the person who is making them. They should not be left at all until finished, because the drifting fabrics from which they are made can get into everything else in the wardrobe. Once they are finished and sprayed with some cheap and very strong setting lotion they can be put out of harm's way, but should be kept standing on something resembling a wig-block. A log of wood or a quart beer bottle are possible wig-stands.

Although wig-making does require a certain amount of skill and care, it is no longer the appalling problem that it was a comparatively few years ago, before the introduction of nylon. There are two essential requirements for an effective wig: first, a wig-block, solid and made of wood, not a hat-stand or anything that is covered with soft material; next sufficient finance to buy switches of nylon hair. These can be bought in any of the cheaper stores and are about 18 in. in length. They are made so that the hair falls from a fold some 3 in. long, and cost about five shillings each. Three switches carefully arranged on a base, which could be anything from a nylon stocking to a thin skull cap, can produce an excellent effect. It is absolutely necessary, however, to have a wig-block on which it can be arranged—the hair spread out, first pinned through to the block and afterwards, when arranged to the satisfaction of the wig-maker, sewn firmly to the 'cap' or stocking (but only where the 3-in. edge exists, for any other sewing must be of a minimum and it is better to use hair clips than to use stitches in most places). The important places to sew are across the forehead and at the back or 'crown' of the head.

If the hair has to be 'set', rollers with a prickly surface must *not* be used; they get inextricably involved with the nylon and ruin it completely. It is not advisable to use Copydex either with this type of 'hair'. Other types of wigs may be made from such materials as horsehair and drainpipe filling, but these take more skill and practice.

Unless the Chinese effect of a completely false beard is required, nylon hair is not for making beards. These are still easiest to manage if the old fashioned crêpe hair is stuck to a gauze base and attached to the face with spirit glue.

48. Young country-women.

49. A.—Showing how a falconer's pouch is attached to his belt.
B.—Showing scabbard, pouch and small purse for coins.
C.—A hunting horn attached to the belt.

CHAPTER 7

Royalty and Nobility

The theatrical use of certain distinguishing clothes for persons of eminence
in moralities was considerable. These distinctive garments in the Middle Ages
varied but slightly throughout Christendom, and normally the materials
which were the most difficult and costly to come by were those which carried
with them a certain elevated significance. The extreme case was the general
use of ermine for the apparel of kings in all European countries. Deep collars
of ermine covering the upper arm and sometimes cut with a scalloped edge,
were worn by both kings and queens for regal occasions (see overleaf). Their
mantles were lined with ermine, but the colours of such mantles seem to have
varied as much as those of their wealthier subjects.

Traditionally regal colours are scarlet and purple and the deep magenta of
the ancients. In theatre directions, scarlet and purple seem to predominate.
In *A Morality of Wisdom: Who is Christ*, which comes from the Macro Plays
(*c.* 1460), edited by F. J. Furnivall and Alfred W. Pollard, the first scene
opens with the following instructions: 'First entered Wisdom in a rich purple
cloth of gold, with a mantle of the same lined with ermine; upon his head a
wig with a fringe on the forehead, a beard of Cyprus gold, curled; a rich
Imperial Crown on his head set with precious stones and pearls. In his left
hand an orb (a ball of gold with a cross on top) and in his right hand a regal
sceptre.'

This certainly gives us a clear picture of a royal figure and one which is
confirmed by the works of the contemporary artists, but instances of other
colours for robes and mantles are to be found everywhere. The 'Imperial
Crown' is illustrated on page 101.

The long robes of counsellors and their head-dress vary considerably, and
there are a dozen instances where certain figures, supposedly representing
authority, are wearing the long gown (based again on a circle or half-circle)
split at the sides with a shoulder-piece added, either a cape or two smaller
half-circles with the straight edge attached from the breast over the shoulder

50. King carrying orb and sceptre and wearing the scalloped
ermine collar peculiar to royalty.

to the base of the scapular (see page 21). Such robes must reach to the ground
to give them full dignity. They should be worn with a hood, and often a hat
as well. The cape and deep collar, sometimes of ermine, which was made with
a curved shoulder seam, could be pulled up over the head, thus forming a
hood and showing a fur 'bib' front.

Uniforms, or similar garments intended to indicate that certain persons
belonged to a king's or nobleman's household, were nearly always parti-
coloured, possibly one half striped, the other plain. This can be seen in a great
many illuminated manuscripts and is often interpreted as a normal costume,
when in truth it was clearly an heraldic emblem to those who designed and
those who saw the illustration at the time.

Originally this convention appeared in its obvious form, in courtiers
wearing parti-coloured tabards designed with heraldic simplicity to make their
household recognisable. Even today this sort of uniform prevails in football
teams, or the colours worn by jockeys. Next we find it in divisions (of woven
materials) into stripes, an easy method of weaving and as effective and indelible
as possible. The fact that such stripes are so often seen in medieval paintings
as diagonal simply indicates that the garment had been cut in the manner
already described (see page 16), semi-circular, circular or shaped on the
diagonal of the material. As usual, shaping and semi-circular folds produce a
more luxurious effect than anything cut on the straight. The King's 'orchestra'
in the Codex of the Manesse family in the University Library, Heidelberg,
printed in facsimile as *Die Minnesinger in Bildern der Manessischen Hande-
schrift*, gives a perfect example of the use of such woven stripes during the
early years of the 14th century. This particular manuscript also indicates how

51. Imperial Crown.

52. Princess with hair free under head-dress. King wearing ermine
cap and gorget. Musician in parti-coloured gown, uniform with
the rest of the orchestra.

well established was the use of heraldry at the time, and something of the variety of musical instruments that were common to the age (see p. 102).

There are a great many morality plays, especially those written in the second half of the 15th century, that are not concerned with the characters with whom we have already become familiar in the mysteries and miracles, but few of them give explicit directions about their costume.

Moralities can be mainly religious, concerned with moral teachings and with the struggle between God and the Devil for the souls of mankind and with the ultimate promise of life hereafter. Plays such as *Everyman*, *Mankind*, *Wisdom* and *The Castle of Perseverance*, all deal with these problems, and require a certain amount of orthodoxy in their dress. But we do find a few delightful exceptions to this rule when the deadly sins are considered as suitable characters to furnish the moral uplift, at least at courts and in the homes of the wealthy.

One of the most diverting of these is Nicole de la Chesnaye's *La Condemnation de Banquet* where gluttony and the diseases which attack the glutton are pitted against each other in actual combat. This play, which may be some years older than the printed edition first published in 1507, was crowded with characters, and the author makes the following introductory explanation of his theme:

'It should be said about this work that there are many names and characters of various illnesses, such as Apoplexy, Epilepsy, Dropsy, Jaundice, Gout and others, to whom I have not always given gender and sex according to the rules of grammar. That is to say that in many places I speak of this or the other personage sometimes in the masculine and sometimes in the feminine, without taking into account the appropriateness of their names or attire, since I intend, with regard to the significance of their names, that their appearance should be more monstrous than human. In the same way, all the characters attending Lady Experience, such as Sobriety, Diet, Bleeding, Pill, and the others, will be in male dress and speak of themselves in the masculine, since they act as officials, serjeants and agents of justice, and undertake many duties that are more suitable to men than to women. And since those works that we call plays or morality plays are not always easy to act or perform publicly to simple people, and since also many people like as much to possess or to hear them read in book form, I have tried to set out this little work in such a way that it should be suitable for production visible to all through characters, gestures and dialogue on the stage or elsewhere, and at the same time so that it can be read in private or alone, as a form of study, pastime or good doctrine.'

He then proceeds to tell his tale and write his play with the precise concern for detail peculiar to playwrights in almost any age. Disner, Soupper and

53. Fool with goose head on the peak of his hood, bells on ears
and on costume. Bauble with bearded face. (Sketch taken from
tapestry in Nancy Museum.)

Bancquet decide to entertain a number of jovial guests who are the sort of
people who have in any age been useful characters to help a party off to a
flying start. Bonne-Campagnie is their leader, and Gourmandise, Friandise,
Passetemps, Je-bois-a'-vous, Je-pleige-d'autant and Accoustumance are in her
train. Disner sets out with a harmless gesture of hospitality but Soupper and

Bancquet scheme to entertain the same guests independently so that they can surfeit them and call in the attentions of all the diseases that were at that time considered the natural rewards of over-eating: Colique, Goutte, Jaunisse, Gravelle, Appoplexie, Ydropsie, Epilence, Pleuresie, Paralisis, Equinancie. During supper these diseases make their appearance in horrid guise but do not seriously damage the guests, though they cause them considerable confusion and discomfort. However, during banquet they renew the onslaught, and only three of the guests escape their fatal attacks: Bonne-Compagnie, Passetemps and Accousyumance. These three seek the help of Dame Experience, to punish Soupper and Bancquet for their evil intentions. Dame Experience calls upon the cures for gluttony—Remede, Secours, Clistre, Sobresse, Saignee, Diette and Pilule—who drag Soupper and Bancquet in chains into court, where a trial scene ensues. At the trial Ypocras and Galien make their appearance and apply classic medical tradition to the judgement. Soupper is condemned to wear handcuffs to stop putting too much on the table and also he is warned to keep his distance from Disner, the time specified being six hours. Bancquet is condemned to be hanged for murder and Diet is chosen as hangman. The final scene is a scaffold with a father-confessor called in as Bancquet's last request.

Throughout the script details concerning the realism of property food, the laying of tables, behaviour of servants and suggestions for both songs and music occur at suitable intervals. There are only a few items of clothing mentioned, but one concerns the donning of the Lombard costume by the fool or 'Vice' when he wants food from the table without being recognised. This may possibly be a topical reference to Louis XII's conquest of Lombardy and the commandeering of great riches from that country. A set of contemporary tapestries illustrating this play is to be seen at the Museum of Nancy in France.

That some attempt at theatre costume was made is quite obvious to us if the tapestries are studied in detail. There are all sorts of fascinating indications of characterisation visible. The diseases that attack the revellers during the banquet are a nightmare assortment of witches and warlocks dressed with weird head-dresses and strangely assorted clothes. Where they appear in the second tapestry they all seem to have the elongated noses and jutting chins which suggest the mask of a Punchinello: a witch-face as old as time, yet 'monstrous as well as human' as suggested in the author's prologue. Some have women's head-dress and wear men's long hose, some have male head-dress and wear skirts; all are armed with an assortment of body armour as well as carrying the weapons suggested in the book.

Here we have a medieval play which calls for all sorts of rich clothing, for excess is the motivating object. It also calls for ingenuity in the use of masks, and could make a fascinating production even today.

The clothes of the wealthy during this time were very much a status symbol, and their peculiar decoration was something to be wondered at by all who saw them. Theirs was a peacock display of colourful richness cut with an apparently reckless grandeur from strange fabrics from foreign lands. The real difference between their clothes and those of the less fortunate was not one of cut, however. We can see pictures of yeomen and poor men wearing semi-circular or even circular cloaks with as much material in them as the magnificently dagged gowns of their lords and masters. But we do not see such men wearing ornate patterns, nor wasting time in cutting the edges of clothes to form leaves and half circles, or other decorated scallops which show a fine lining and make it quite clear that the wearer was in a position to have two fabrics rather than one for his dress.

Fineness of fabrics and ornate design immediately imply that such things were not manufactured in the north, neither in France, Holland nor Britain. Their use was therefore confined to a class who could pay the high prices demanded by the merchants who in their turn had travelled many hundreds

54. Dagged short gown and shoes.

of miles by sea, braving many dangers in order to bring such rich merchandise from the countries where silk was manufactured.

There was almost a fabled romance attached to the owners of such stuffs, for the Middle Ages were a very real setting for Aladdin's cave with its rich hoards of sparkling jewels, bales of cloth of gold and priceless silks which could, because of their fineness, be drawn through a ring. Pirates of the time risked everything in their attempts to despoil a rich merchant ship, knowing full well that there would be no difficulty in selling at any price they cared to ask the oriental stuffs and precious gee-gaws which were so coveted in the northern hemisphere where the natural fabric was wool or linen, and the natural dyes vegetable and earth. Thus rich clothes were very definitely foreign, outlandish or 'peregrine' as it was then called.

Fine fabrics came from the south, and those that had made the longest journey were the most coveted. Their names alone carried the full flavour of the age of romance: samites of lovely silk shot through with gold; sendals so heavy that they could be used for banners; Cyprus silks decorated with gold and silver; satins and velvets from Spain, Venice or Naples; cloth of gold and silver from Persia and Arabia said to be worth a king's ransom; damasks from Damascus; jewel-studded fragments of silk supposedly torn from the robes of slaughtered infidels. These formed a glittering hoard of riches to decorate the wealthy and make them immediately different from their own countrymen.

It is comparatively easy, then, to imitate the richness of the time if we concentrate on the foreign element in the designs themselves. Designs which were carried out in Persia or Arabia or even Spain and Portugal were often inspired by the semi-tropical foliage of those countries, the exotic fauna and flora of another world, and influenced also by the geometric Muslim patterns. Such objects as pomegranates and pineapples, peacocks, pelicans and flamingoes, lions, elephants and tigers and numerous other foreign motifs of fascinating and exotic life decorated the garments of the nobility and the wealthy merchantmen.

Dyes of rare shades and brilliant colour contrasts also came from overseas, and such colour also was characteristic of the wealthy. Rich stuffs were for the rich, simple homespun for the middle class, and rags and tags for the poor. A perfectly simple and recognisable division of status in society.

There seems to have been every reason why there should have been an outcry in the hearts of men who wanted to accuse an upper class of extravagances to which they themselves could never attain, and such an outcry has been recorded for posterity in the poetry and moralities of the Middle Ages. It is therefore necessary for theatre designers to understand something of the main characteristics which immediately indicated that a man was a 'Man of Substance' that Worldly and Covetousness in *The Castle of Perseverance*, for instance,

55. Three kings bearing gifts.

must each be recognisable in his particular role, must look rich almost beyond the dreams of avarice, and this can be engineered so easily for theatre purposes if these particular garments are of the 'peregrine' caste.

It is also useful to remember that towards the end of the 14th century when clothes were either really voluminous or extremely scanty, there was a fantastic fashion for calling attention to them by the wearing of bells as a decoration. Belts hung with little gold or silver bells, a shoulder belt with larger bells, a necklet of bells all decorated with fine workmanship or damascene, and possibly even studded with precious stones. It was a sign of rank to wear great chains of gold and belts of fine leather and metal work, in fact to draw attention to oneself not only by the obvious grandeur of a garment, but also by the noise it made, the rustle and swish augmented by the tinkling of a hundred little bells, the flash of jewels, the glitter of gold chains and the clank of swords. All these things added to the 'presence', instilled jealousy and awe into the beholder, and made the wearer conscious of the figure that he hoped to make.

Riches and poverty were then poles apart, and the contrast should not be difficult to attain.

Fabric designs which give a feeling for medieval pageantry and exotic splendour are not too easy to obtain today. There are still a few traditional ogee patterns to be found amongst furnishing fabrics which give an impression of damask, but the colours so often lack distinction and because of their function as furnishing fabrics they all tend to be indefinite. Definition was an important factor in the original designs because they were expressly woven to attract attention, to be marvels of colour and texture that would make the would-be purchaser spellbound by their rare beauty. Often, again, furnishing fabrics are extremely difficult to make up because of the looseness of the weave and the amount of fraying that takes place as soon as they are cut on the cross of the material.

For a garment that should look rich in design and does not have to be cleaned, patterns or designs cut out in velvet and stuck to the main fabric with Copydex can be extremely effective. These will not clean or wash, however, and should be carried out with this drawback in mind. Hessian makes an excellent background for such an experiment, especially if it is in its natural shade and not dyed; there is a goldish quality about it that catches the light and gives an illusion of richness. Velvets used for the stuck-on design should be cotton; the cheapest type of velveteen, though preferably not corded, is better than anything else because it does not fray out as quickly as silk does. It is as well when using hessian, to tack down the hem carefully before stitching in the lining because of its ability to fray, stretch and generally misbehave.

Probably the best possible method of obtaining the right sort of effect in design is to get the material screen-printed. The process is comparatively simple and almost any art school will give the necessary instruction to those who are interested. Screen-printing is both quick and immensely effective. Whole colour schemes can in this way be worked out without fear of clashing or unsympathetic colours. The very cheapest fabrics can be used, even such materials as Bolton sheeting or unbleached canvas. The ground can in fact be practically covered by the design yet still give just that necessary subdued colour

56. Parti-coloured uniform similar to that worn in 'The Court of the King's Bench' early 15th century.

to throw up the brightness of the surface dyes. Simple instructions for other types of textile printing can be found, for example, in the Dryad publications, but because of its size nothing is so immediately effective as the use of a screen.

Stencilling and hand-painting are also practicable, but both take a great deal more time, and stencilling in particular cannot be rushed; there are too many things to go wrong from the slipping paper to the paint running underneath and making a complete mess of a repeat pattern. Lino-block printing is useful for borders which repeat on a straight line only. Any curved edge can present difficulties.

Wherever 'jewels' have to be used on fabrics, it is as well to first look for those which have holes pierced in them already. There is no foolproof method of sticking a jewel on to a frabric that moves, though this can be done in a very temporary manner with Bostik. If the ornaments have no holes, a piece of black net is quite useful—just lay it over the jewel and stitch round making a little pocket for it; the net cover does not unduly detract from the glitter, though it must necessarily dim it a little. Sequins should always be covered in this way because of their metallic quality, and so should foil of any sort—gold, silver or coloured. Stage lighting tends to pick out tiny pinpoints of light which flash and twinkle at unexpected moments in a most distracting way; it is in fact sometimes impossible to keep one's attention upon the acting if a tiny 'Tinkerbell' light is rushing about the set, or a mere pinpoint of brilliant star-like quality flashing on and off at the actor's slightest movement.

One of the many reasons why theatre costume of the Middle Ages can be so very lovely and worth while is because of its contemporary contrasts; on the one side the soft earth shades, russets and greens worn by the country folk, textures of coarse fabrics held in place by leather belts and jerkins; white wimples and simple arrangements of various head scarves. On the other side, grandeur and exaggeration; brilliant dyes, contrasting colours, flashes of gold and silver, the use of parti-coloured garments, heraldic symbols and gigantic patterns; head-dress of exaggerated and fantastic shapes and sizes, sweeping trains and dragging sleeves, nothing in fact that was to be mistaken for the simple dress of the lesser man.

Of such costumes where time and finance are of secondary importance there are wonderful examples in the famous 'Les très riches heures du duc de Berry' which is in the Musée Condé, Chantilly, but obtainable in post-cards from the Louvre. Their construction is something of a mystery, their colouring of exquisite beauty, their head-dress and dagged sleeves a bewildering fantasy of pattern. Here we can see the use of bells, collars, belts and hanging streamers of weighted golden flowers; parti-colouring, mi-parti hose, fur-edged gowns, embroidered decorations in gold; hats and caps, a rich variety of fanciful hoods and false sleeves hanging like cloaks from the shoulders. Practically every book on costume has used these lavish examples to show the courtly costumes of the early 15th century. For pageantry they would be splendid, as indeed they were, but there are comparatively few possibilities of using such splendour in the normal run of medieval plays. Nor—and this is a particularly important point—is there sufficient room for such clothes in any restricted acting area. The effect of trains and floating sleeves is utterly ruined if cramped for space; unless the whole sweep of such gowns can be seen, they are an encumbrance to the actors themselves and a booby trap for their followers.

Index